Negotiate Your Way
to Financial Success

Negotiate Your Way To Financial Success

RONALD J. POSLUNS

G. P. Putnam's Sons
New York

G. P. Putnam's Sons
Publishers Since 1838
200 Madison Avenue
New York, NY 10016

Designed by Rhea Braunstein

Library of Congress Cataloging-in-Publication Data

Posluns, Ronald J.
  Negotiate your way to financial success.

  1. Negotiation in business. I. Title.
HD58.6.P67   1987   658.1'5   87-2408
ISBN 0-399-13239-2

Printed in the United States of America
1   2   3   4   5   6   7   8   9   10

Acknowledgments

There is no more difficult and humbling a task than having to spill your guts on paper by taking your innermost thoughts, meshing them with real-life situations in which you have been involved, and then writing them down for all the world to read.

This book could never have been written without the help of Judy Linden, my editor, who went far beyond the call of duty to press for even more material and massage the book into a presentable format, and William Reiss, my agent and friend, who had faith in me even before this project was conceived.

Niel Shister, the editor of *Atlanta Magazine,* helped with the organization and editing of the manuscript. His editorial instincts and concern with making sure my ideas were clearly expressed helped to make this book better.

Of course I must thank Arlene, my wife of twenty-one years, for typing the endless drafts; Mark, my sixteen-year-old son, with his magnetic personality; and Lynn, the creative one, who never ceases to amaze me with her new insight. To these three, I can only say thank you for the long hours I took away from enjoying their companionship.

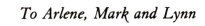
To Arlene, Mark and Lynn

CONTENTS

Negotiate Your Way
to Financial Success

I'VE DONE IT—
SO CAN YOU!

THE HOT TALK these days is about doing deals. According to reports in the newspapers and on television, the brightest and the best on the college campuses want to go to Wall Street to do deals; in Hollywood the deal is as much a work of art as the finished movie; big business, which used to be a matter of producing goods and then marketing them, seems increasingly to be about putting together new companies and spinning off unwanted ones. Even in our ordinary lives, especially in light of the new savings, investing, and spending strategies necessitated by the new tax laws, we find ourselves, when we buy a house or take out a loan, engaged in dealmaking.

There is something that all deals and dealmakers have in common: *negotiation*. Although a lot of us don't realize it, we are involved every day in all sorts of negotiations. Sometimes it is with our spouse or children, our employers or employees, the mechanic at the garage, or even the clerk in the store. And while most of us, in these daily encounters, don't think of ourselves as big-time dealmakers, the skills and arts of the hotshot wheeler-dealers—the people who negotiate for a living—are just as applicable to us as to the famous financiers you read about in the business pages.

How well you understand what you're doing, how conscious you are of the strategy and tactics of negotiation, will influence how well you do your deals. Whether you are seeking to attract millions of dollars of venture capital to fund your entrepreneurial dream of a lifetime, or trying to get the big raise you deserve from a reluctant boss, the same principles of negotiation apply.

This book is about how to negotiate for financial success—your financial success! I am a professional negotiator. People hire me to help them make their deals, to sit down across the table with somebody and hammer out the details of a bargain in which dollars and cents, sometimes in large amounts, are at stake. The lessons I have learned, the tricks of the trade I've picked up along the way, are presented in this book. By mastering them you can be assured that you'll be able to accomplish through negotiation things you never before dreamed possible. That might mean anything from negotiating to buy a piece of property with no cash down to getting desirable fringe benefits from your next job to securing favorable terms in a loan agreement.

Once you learn my strategies, my ploys, and my winning game-plans, you will recognize that your goals are realistically achievable. I have attained them all. I have

- bought a home with 100% financing, low interest costs, and 75% lower closing costs
- doubled my take-home pay without an increase in salary
- gone to college for free

- reduced my insurance costs by 50%
- earned 15% interest on bank accounts
- started a business with no money down
- signed a lease with no deposits
- earned 40% on investments
- settled insurance claims without a hassle

There is nothing magical about negotiating. It doesn't require supernatural gifts of intelligence, courage, or raw nerve. It is no more and no less than another form of gamesmanship. Sure, it's complicated. It also requires patience and discipline and calm judgment. But these are habits that can be formed. Like golf or tennis, negotiating for financial success requires replacing bad habits with good ones; like hunting or chess it involves strategies and tactics, traps and gambits, lying in wait for the opportune moment to strike. Like bartering it requires mutual cooperation to achieve shared objectives.

But what it doesn't require is brilliance. You will need a plan of action involving lots of preparation and study—there is no substitute for doing your homework! It also requires a spirit of trust (because it takes two to make a deal) along with a degree of cynicism, because you shouldn't believe the other person too much. Finally, negotiating requires a personal style that is partly theater and partly sincerity. There will be moments to be tough and moments to be sympathetic. I'm fond of saying that I am definitely not a saint when I negotiate. I yell, scream, and pound the table on occasion, yet after the deal has been done, I always have time for good fellowship.

I wrote this book to make you aware of all the opportunities in your life for doing better every time you make a deal. I'll identify all the negotiable items in different types of financial situations and explain the key steps in the negotiation process, from strategy to execution. Become familiar with my approach and you'll have the negotiating edge every time, everywhere!

There's nothing I can do that you can't do. My approach is eminently teachable because, as you'll see, it is eminently rational. The fundamentals are basic and unchangeable. Anybody of average intelligence can quickly grasp them. So whether you want to learn how to do multimillion-dollar deals or just get the best price on a new car from a surly salesman, the approach in this book will help you achieve your goals. I'm tough, I admit it, and I advocate a strong, hardheaded approach. But that doesn't mean being petty, bullheaded, or arrogant. If anything, the good negotiator is just the opposite—humble in dedication to the craft he or she practices. The approach I advocate may produce some tense moments and strained situations, but it offends no one.

And, most important, it produces substantial financial rewards. Every time! What I have done, you can do too.

1

REAPING THE FINANCIAL FRUITS

LEE IACOCCA, Chairman of Chrysler Corporation, earned more than $37.5 million in salary and gained $15.5 million in stock options over the past five years, after having earned only one dollar in 1980 during Chrysler's brush with bankruptcy. Early on in his tenure, when things looked most bleak, he agreed to take a dollar as his annual salary. It was a dramatic gesture. But if the company turned around the way he expected, or at least was hoping, he would earn a small fortune in stock options and deferred benefits. In essence, Iacocca was leveraging his annual salary against the possibility of much greater gain. He persuaded his employers that such an arrangement was to their mutual interest; moreover, he defied conventional corporate behavior by working under this arrangement. (Quick—can you name one other Chairman-CEO whose salary is currently one dollar?) Iacocca was in effect negotiating the present against the future, willing to put himself on the line, thereby serving as an example to others, but in a manner that would put him in a position to receive ample reward. You know the rest of the story.

21

Another person who stands out in my personal Hall of Fame is Beth Swann, the mother of my son's best friend. Beth was a talented interior designer who had never really practiced in her own right but was primed to go into business when the right opportunity appeared. This situation surfaced, and Beth purchased a home-decorating company for $70,000. She negotiated only $10,000 as a down payment, plus the promise to pay the balance out of earnings. This meant in effect that if there were no earnings, and the business failed to perform, she would be free to defer the balance of her debt obligation. Beth turned out to be an absolutely first-rate businesswoman; she established her reputation in an area where a boom in home building was under way. Her business flourished, so much so that a national furniture retailer sought to buy her out eight or nine years later. She agreed to their offer of $650,000. Think about what she was able to accomplish: for an initial investment of $10,000 plus lots of talent and hard work she was eventually able to realize well over half a million dollars. Talk about leverage!

Such financial rewards were obtained by winging it, with no well-conceived game plan, right? Wrong. Both these people were successful because they knew how to negotiate tough.

OPTIONS

Be realistic. People don't come up to you out of the blue offering spectacular financial opportunities. When was the last time your boss called you into his or her office to give you a big unexpected raise? Has your banker ever offered you a loan below the prime rate? Do you recall one instance when your landlord offered you equity in the property you were renting? Ever? I doubt it.

But that doesn't mean these things—and lots more— can't happen. They do and they will if you learn how to negotiate! Don't expect the heavens to open up one day and shower you with bounty—you have to seed the clouds and make the rain. That's what negotiation is all about— making things happen that otherwise wouldn't occur. In order to do this, you have to know what to ask for and how to ask. You need to learn to think creatively about your options.

You are rarely if ever locked into a situation. You always have options. Take for example the act of buying a house. You can get a conventional mortgage, a loan in which the property does not serve as collateral, or a loan in which it does. You can borrow from a bank, a private lender, or even the seller of the property. In virtually any situation— even adverse ones such as when you're facing foreclosure or the loss of a job—there exists a slew of different options and opportunities.

If I had to name one quality that distinguishes negotiators from non-negotiators it would be the ability to recognize options. Negotiators are able to look beyond the immediate situation to consider the broader implications of a potential arrangement. They ask themselves, What if we offer X instead of Y and then ask the other side to throw Z into the deal? Negotiators are aware of the ongoing presence of options and seek to exploit all possibilities to their own advantage. Non-negotiators think somehow the rules of the game have been written in stone and one is obliged to follow them as they have always been followed (for example, you buy a house with a mortgage obtained from a bank). Trust me—nine times out of ten you'll find flexibility in a situation if you look for it; once you find it, you instantly have the negotiator's edge.

OPPORTUNITIES

Financial opportunities are a part of our everyday lives. Just like Iacocca and Beth Swann, you need to train yourself to recognize potential negotiating situations. I have trained myself to always be primed to spot them. *If money is involved in a situation, it is a potential negotiating opportunity.* Once you grow used to thinking creatively in negotiating situations, you will find all kinds of possibilities open to you. Here are just a few:

• You can negotiate a zero-balance checking account, with no service charge, plus a money market account that will pay you interest until the funds are transferred to the checking account to cover specific checks. The combination of negotiated money-market rates, zero service charges, and timing the withdrawal of funds to coincide with the clearing of the check could result in a return of 15% on funds in your bank accounts.

• You can negotiate to buy a house at the lowest possible price and then further reduce the costs of financing below market rates in your community.

• You can negotiate to significantly increase your take-home pay with no increase in salary or fringe benefits.

• You can negotiate to sell part of the possible income generated by a stock's dividends and capital gains in return for immediate cash and still retain possession of the stock.

• You can negotiate a greater share of profits than your partners even though you all invested the same amount of dollars.

• You can negotiate to have the landlord hand *you* a check when you sign a lease instead of vice versa.

• You can negotiate to acquire a company many times larger than your own, using the cash flow of the acquired firm to fund the purchase.

• You can negotiate directly or through an arbitrator with the largest companies in the world, such as General Motors, and obtain a favorable settlement of your claim regarding defects in their product even though millions of others are unwilling to challenge the firm or have been unsuccessful in similar attempts to do so.

Every negotiation represents new options and trade-offs, and every option is a new opportunity for obtaining greater financial rewards.

THE GAME PLAN

It all comes down to this: *Negotiate for what you want or be prepared to settle for less.* But to negotiate, to know what's at stake and recognize the opportune moment to seize it, you need to develop a plan that defines your goals and your strategy to achieve these goals. Before you get into the heated combat of the negotiating, take stock and decide on your priorities and objectives. *Know what you want to get out of a negotiation before going into one.* A good negotiator knows where he or she wants to end up even if he isn't entirely sure how to get there. Get yourself a pad of paper and write down exactly what you're trying to accomplish. That way, as the bargaining process unfolds, you'll have a clear-eyed focus of your destination.

Luck has little to do with successful negotiation. Planning, on the other hand, is critical. Some people complain about never being at the right place at the right time to make the right deal. I confess I have little patience with them. I like to repeat the comment Branch Rickey, the legendary baseball genius who negotiated Jackie Robinson's admission into the big leagues, had made about being lucky. He once said, "Good luck is the residue of design." Translation: "good fortune" happens to those with a goal and a plan to achieve it. When you know what you're looking for, you'll recognize the right cards when fate hands them down.

CREATIVITY

You have to be creative in thinking about your situation in order to be a successful negotiator. You'll want to think in terms of leverage, which is like figuring out a way to make one dollar do the work of ten dollars. Leveraged financial rewards are what you want to go after in your demands. You do this by negotiating to get *immediate dollar concessions,* then *leveraging* these concessions to get you a share of your opponent's rewards. For example, you may want to negotiate participation in the ownership of a business and a share in its annual profits (immediate dollar concessions) and thus be in a position to receive subsequent capital gains if the firm is sold (opponent's rewards).

In every negotiating situation think about what you have to offer that the other side needs. It may be cash, reliability, talent, or the promise of security. When proposing any deal, both sides will weigh the pros and cons, size up what is in the deal for them and how to get the most from it. The challenge of thinking creatively as a negotiator is to figure out your strengths in every given situation, what you have that the other side wants—and then leverage that strength to its maximum advantage.

Thinking creatively as a negotiator means

- constructing a proposal in which both sides benefit;
- persuading the other side that by granting your demands they, too, will profit;
- daring to envision bold results—huge pay raises, great leasing deals, advantageous loans—and then structuring a deal that makes such results acceptable to the other side;
- being willing to be a nonconformist—just because everybody else is doing a certain kind of deal a certain way doesn't mean you should too; instead, rethink everything about the deal, right down to the fundamental assumptions and premises;
- coming up with options: Get your new landlord who is eager to lease you an expensive new apartment to

buy you out of your old one, or have your employer create a scholarship plan for your children's college education rather than give you a raise in taxable dollars.

After all the cardinal principles have been learned, options explored, and your opponent's concessions leveraged, there is one last thing to know about negotiating: it is financially rewarding. Why should you settle for less when you can negotiate for greater financial rewards? No reason!

2

NEGOTIATING TO WIN: THE FUNDAMENTALS

TO NEGOTIATE and win, you don't have to be a great charmer—just a consummate, steady planner with a professional approach. Sure, you must begin with an attitude that exudes *confidence* (always believe you can win) and *credibility* (so your opponent also believes that you can win), but this is just the starting point. As important as they are, attitude and credibility only improve the climate for negotiating success. They intensify the mix. It is the winning game plan, though, that gives you the negotiating edge, every time.

To become a winning negotiator, you have to be aware of what you're doing and why. The first step is to learn the fundamentals. Negotiating can be broken down into basic and easily learned components. The building blocks of negotiating are simple: a credible style, selectivity in choosing your spots and knowing industry norms, a set of consistently reliable rules to follow for every negotiating situation, a well-stocked arsenal of techniques to deploy when you enter the actual bargaining sessions, and a winning game plan.

A CREDIBLE STYLE

Negotiations are based on trust. You have to believe that the other side is willing and able to do what it promises; they must believe the same of you. Regardless of the tactics and ploys you use during the actual bargaining, there has to be this mutual confidence in the good faith of each side or there is no basis for doing any kind of deal. So I always stress the importance of approaching negotiations with a positive attitude. You need to project a personal style that exudes confidence and inspires credibility. You always need to believe in your heart that you can win, because if you don't think so, no one else will either, least of all your opponent. And you need to behave in a way that makes this belief credible.

As you begin a negotiation, size up your opponent on two counts: confidence and credibility. Does he or she act like someone who is in control of the situation? Is he empowered to deviate from the normal rules? Does he seem sure or uncertain of himself? Most important, make sure that your opponent has *the authority to negotiate and implement the terms of the deal.* Too many people waste time talking to clerks who just shuffle papers and act as gatekeepers. Compile all this information in your mental databank for future reference. Assume your opponent is judging you the same way. So make sure you are sending out the right signals of confidence and credibility. Even if you're a tad nervous about what is about to transpire, don't let it show. People deal differently with winners than with losers.

Let me pass along one of my favorite gems, which has

worked well over the years. I grew up believing that a person's word was his or her bond, and that's how I negotiate. Not everybody agrees with this belief anymore, especially as deals become increasingly complicated and subject to last-minute changes. Still, no matter how many lawyers earn big fees drawing up the contract, no matter how many clauses there are and how many loopholes you close, the merit of a deal still comes down to the intentions of each party. Do they really intend to honor the agreement? You'll never know until the last dollar is paid out. Trust has to start somewhere, however, so let it begin with you.

There will be times when you will be tempted to back out on your word. I know. I learned firsthand how hard it can be to say no to temptation, especially since it cost me $20,000 out-of-pocket. I was in the process of opening an office in Detroit in conjunction with some work I was scheduled to do. On the day the lease was scheduled to be signed, I learned, not entirely to my satisfaction, that my situation had changed dramatically and there was no longer any reason for me to be in Detroit. But one month earlier I had agreed to lease the space. I had given my word to the landlord, who had refurbished the office and later that afternoon would sit across from me with his attorney to sign the lease. I had two choices: walk away from the deal or honor it. As someone who earns his living negotiating situations in which others are expected to keep their word, I decided there was no alternative for me but to keep my part of the bargain. The deal went down. Fortunately, I knew (the landlord didn't) that I was able to sublease the facility to another tenant and also was paid $25,000 for the furnishings. More important, when I opened an office in Florida, the same landlord (who I knew had a choice facility I wanted) welcomed me with open arms and a sweetheart of a deal. A good negotiator should rely on preparation and quick wits, not sham and duplicity. Nothing comes back to haunt you faster than the reputation of not honoring your commitments.

PICKING YOUR SPOTS CAREFULLY

This is the second key to becoming a good negotiator. Don't rush out and take on everyone. The more time you spend considering alternatives before entering into a negotiating situation, the further ahead you'll be. Remember, being a skillful negotiator doesn't mean you do a *lot* of deals, only that you do *good* ones.

Picking your negotiating spots is like buying a used car. There are many models on the lot, yet obviously you can't purchase them all. You need to choose carefully the one that best meets your requirements and specifications. Then you have to check it out. Only then are you ready to get down to negotiating. If you fail to do this, if you impulsively buy the first car to catch your fancy because you like its color, you'll quickly discover it is a clunker. Don't blame the salesman and don't call him a crook. Call yourself a fool. The dealer had done his homework—he knew the value of what he was selling. You may have bargained like a wizard and negotiated like a genius, but you were still a loser in the end because you didn't carefully select your situation.

Obviously you are likely to enter into negotiations for something considerably more significant than a used car, but the principle of selectivity still applies.

Negotiate only those deals in which you have a good chance of success. Do this by establishing your minimum demands right at the outset. If you can't achieve these, then the deal is a clunker, no matter how many assorted fringe benefits you can negotiate. For instance, what's the good of getting a fancy car with a fantastic audio system and glove-leather interior at an inflated price if the power train is so badly designed that it keeps breaking down? Your minimum demand in this case would be a car with a reliable engine, not a lot of fancy accessories.

Let's say you're looking for space for your business and you're shopping around town to find the best deal. Fix your minimum demands. If it's $10 a square foot with six months' free rent, don't waste time trying to negotiate with a landlord who won't drop his price below $15 a foot, no matter how many added perks he throws in. Why continue talking to someone who will lend you only $25,000 when you need at least $100,000?

Break off negotiations quickly in such cases. You'll save time. And you'll demonstrate that you do business differently from most other people because you know how to bargain for your own requirements rather than passively accepting somebody else's. Remember—there always will be another landlord or another lender around the bend, so *don't rush yourself into the wrong deal.* The moment you start thinking an opportunity is your last shot at something, you have significantly weakened your effectiveness as a negotiator!

By establishing your "minimum agenda" you will accomplish several other things. You will force yourself to conduct a fundamental analysis of your financial situation to determine what is and what isn't negotiable. You will insert an additional "control" into your mind-set, imposing a discipline on yourself that forces you to be clearer and more precise about your goals and options.

As you find yourself in more sensitive, sophisticated situations, your private information will become increasingly more valuable. You may for example try to fund an entrepreneurial project through an investment banker or venture-capital firm. In such instances it is to your advantage to guard your proprietary information until you are sure you and the other side are in the same negotiating ball park. Establish as soon as you can whether the other side can meet your minimum demands concerning money and terms. If they can't, don't share your business plan with them! More than one horror story has been told about brilliant ideas being stolen by supposedly trustworthy financial analysts for lending institutions who were privy to confidential data.

INDUSTRY NORMS

Another aspect of choosing your situations carefully relates to the norms of the industry with which you're involved. Determine the general guidelines of that industry, then focus in on your own specific set of demands. You will be amazed at what you can ask for—and get—if you know what others are asking for and getting. The entertainment industry is filled with examples of what would be outrageous requests for most of us, but in Hollywood they pass for the norm. Take the deal Blake Edwards negotiated for the movie *Victor/Victoria*. He received one million dollars for producing it, two hundred thousand dollars for the screenplay, four thousand dollars per week living expenses during production and, as a final little goody, ten first-class round-trip air tickets between London and New York. Sports is another example. When the USFL was trying to establish itself as a viable competitor to the NFL, Herschel Walker, the widely sought runner from Georgia, was able to get himself a guaranteed multimillion-dollar contract. Obviously we're not all Blake Edwardses or Herschel Walkers, but if we know what the superstars are getting in our own specific industries, then we'll be better equipped to structure our own set of minimum demands. I've never heard of an opponent in a negotiation saying, "You should ask for more, your demands are way out of whack with the norm," but I have heard about lots of deals where some poor innocent, unaware of what was going on around him, accepted terms far below what he might have requested just because he was unaware of what others, in situations comparable to his, were getting.

Okay, you've got the proper attitude—confident and credible. And you've done your homework—compiled your minimum demands and shopped around to find someone who is prepared to meet them. Now the fun begins. You're ready to negotiate.

SEVEN GOLDEN RULES

At the heart of every winning game plan is a self-imposed set of goals and strategies. Over the course of my career, however, I have developed a set of consistently reliable rules or guidelines that provide a framework within which you can execute your game plan. These rules apply to every financial negotiating situation.

Rule 1: Negotiate Tough.

Ian Sinclair, a prominent international businessman who has negotiated some classic deals as chairman of the multinational corporate giant Canadian Pacific and director of twenty-three other firms, sums it up like this: You can't be popular all the time; as long as the deal is fair for both sides, there is nothing wrong with getting the edge in any deal. Remember, you don't get any extra financial rewards by being a cream puff.

Don't confuse "tough" with arrogant, rude, bullheaded, or ruthless. There's no reason why a successful negotiator also can't be polite. Indeed, good manners and decorum almost always work to your favor in the end. "Tough" means sticking to your guns, letting the other side know you mean business, being unafraid to ask for extra concessions. Command respect! It produces better results.

Rule 2: "God Is in the Details."

Roberto Goizueta, the Chairman of Coca-Cola, tells this story. He was negotiating for the acquisition of Columbia Pictures and the deal had reached the stage where contracts were on the table. He informed his bargaining team that he wanted to be advised on the specifics of each element in the contract—just exactly what they meant in real terms. "You mean all the details?" he was asked in horror. That is precisely what he meant, citing the dictum of the famous philosopher Nietzsche, "God is in the details."

The success of your negotiation lies in the details of the deal. Go through them, subpoint by subpoint. Wherever there is an item that is up for grabs, go for it! For example, take the repayment schedule of a loan: monthly, quarterly, annually? Structure the terms to your advantage. You're buying a house—who will pay for the clean-up service before you move in? You're working out the terms of a new employment contract—who will pay for the service and repairs of the company car you are going to get? Assume nothing!

In every negotiation there are items that are virtually left on the table, concessions that the other side is willing to give up because they appear to cost nothing or are apparently inconsequential to the deal at hand. Ask for them! They are yours for the taking.

On your side, consider no item as insignificant. The least you should do is negotiate hard on every specific item, especially the smaller ones, in order to wear down your opponent's stamina when the major issues are at stake.

Rule 3: Focus on the Rewards.
Results are all that count.

On one occasion I represented a client in dealings with a banker in upstate New York. For fifteen minutes this guy huffed and puffed, pounding on the table, ranting and raving that my client had personally insulted him after twenty years of doing business together by asking for better terms on a major loan. We refused to take the bait. After he finished his diatribe we remained silent, perhaps for five full minutes. He settled down. And we had the advantage, since he had played his emotional card to no avail. We let him do his thing and then we did ours, negotiating twenty-four favorable changes in the loan agreement.

Rule 4: Avoid Ultimatums.

Don't give your opponent *ultimatums,* give him *choices.* When you back somebody up against the wall, demanding a yes or a no, it's like cornering a wild animal—you just can't predict his or her reactions. Even if, in response to an ultimatum, your opponent accedes to your terms, the ill will you have sown may later—even years later—come back to haunt you when he decides not to honor his side of the deal. How do you avoid ultimatums? Never give your opponent the chance to say no, but instead give him assorted choices so he can say yes to something. Let him see the advantages of dealing with you; don't stick a rifle to his head and say, "Hands up or I'll shoot!"

What about the other side of the coin, when somebody confronts *you* with an ultimatum? "Take it or leave it right now!" he insists. I would advise you, unconditionally, to leave it on those terms. A deal that can't survive another day of indecision surely can't be the basis for a long-term relationship. But sometimes you can turn an ultimatum into a bargaining advantage. Offer to take it with the provision that an added bonus be thrown into the equation, a reward for apparently acquiescing to an ultimatum (although in fact you haven't backed down but have deflected it to your own advantage).

Rule 5: Nothing in Negotiations is According to Hoyle.

There are no established rules; anything goes. I knew a very good negotiator who was also a pipe smoker; in a particularly sticky moment he would elaborately light his pipe, stalling for time, buying himself a minute or two to compose his response. Here's a ploy I've been known to use when the circumstances are right. You find yourself up against a blue-chip snob, the proverbial silk-stocking aristocrat who thinks he or she is superior to you. For the moment I let him think that. At a critical juncture of the negotiations I purposely drop a file or my briefcase on the floor, scattering papers everywhere. I drop to all fours to pick up the mess, looking like a klutz and lulling my opponent into even more smug self-confidence. Or I make a mess with my fountain pen—which is one of the reasons I still use one—apologetically mopping up while the other guy laughs to himself (while I set him up for the kill). The purpose of these theatrics is to make your opponent underestimate you, to keep him or her off balance.

Rule 6: Find Your Opponent's Pressure Points.

You can do this through research. For example, if you are negotiating to buy a business from someone, determine if he has to sell it before December 31 for tax purposes. You can do this by suggesting that you meet, say, on January 5, to discuss the terms. The response will tell you what you want to know. Or if you are negotiating to buy a house, find out if the owner is selling because he or she needs quick cash to pay debts. You can learn this by getting a credit report and calling his bank to see if he has any notes coming due. You would be surprised how much information you can gather with a little effort. If you discover that your opponent is facing a deadline, you can exploit this pressure point by stalling right up to the last possible moment, wearing away the clock by dealing with secondary matters until, as the final hour nears, you begin to focus on your main goals. Your adversary will be all the more eager to agree. Or, if you find out that your opponent has a sales quota to fill, you can use this to your advantage. It's true what they say about lots of salespeople—they will make much sweeter deals at the end of a month than at the beginning. And, if you discover that your opponent has immediate, up-front cash needs, trade off the short-term cash for significant long-term concessions. It pays to probe your opponent to determine his or her vulnerable points and then structure your negotiating stance appropriately.

Rule 7: Control the Negotiation.

Get the bargaining process on your terms. If there's a choice between "your place or mine," consider the implications carefully. You have a turf advantage at home, but when you're "away" you can leave the table in mock outrage. You make the choice. Control the negotiation by getting your opponent to follow your game plan, not his.

A good way to gain control is by letting the other side prepare the working document under discussion. They will be happy to do so, mistakenly believing this gives them an edge. Whether it's a lease or an employment contract, you will then have an itemization of what they are looking to obtain and the numbers they attach to those items. You'll also know what they hope to leave out of the deal, through what's been omitted in the document.

Now you're ready to negotiate! Begin with the larger items first, the ones that represent the greatest percentage of the total financial package. Then move on to lesser ones. Remember, if your opponent is a pro, he'll be trying to get you to reverse this order.

I was once asked to negotiate the accommodations for a large convention that was to take place in Florida during the high season, when room rates were the most expensive. I was able to dominate the negotiating process this way: I simply refused to discuss the specific dates we wanted until we had agreed on a room rate and assorted other rates (banquets, entertainment, and such). I made it clear that the total profits to the hotel would more than offset the seasonal differential in room rates. Then, and only then, were we ready to talk about dates. I got the ones I wanted at the room rates I wanted.

Major institutional investors in real estate projects understand how to control negotiations. They become "partners" with a builder, allowing him or her to assemble the property, plan the development, oversee the construction, and market the finished product. They have structured the deal, though, controlling the negotiation process so that the bulk of the risk is one-sided, falling on the developer. The institution provides the money, reduces the interest rate, and defers principal payments in exchange for a kicker— equity in the project and a share of future rental income. If the project leases out quickly, no problem. But if it doesn't, and the builder can't service his debt with rent payments, he loses his equity participation in the project he made happen! I feel sorry for such developers, but not pity; they should have controlled the negotiation.

These were my Seven Golden Rules. You violate any one of them at your own risk; if you violate too many, you may well find yourself out of the game. I say this not to scare you, only to underscore the importance of a planned, disciplined approach to negotiating. There are moments for inspired brilliance, but you must have your fundamentals well established in order to exploit such moments. A lot of us wish we could hit tennis shots with the improvised genius of John McEnroe, but few fully appreciate just how well he does the fundamentals: getting his racket back early, taking that extra step to get to the ball, positioning himself properly on the court. The same is true when you negotiate for financial success. Take care of the basics and the basics will take care of you.

A WELL-STOCKED ARSENAL

There is a rhythm and tempo to any negotiation, and the person who can seize the opportunity to impose his or her own design at those moments has the edge. I like to regard these tactics as the arsenal of negotiating. They tend to be less fixed and hard-edged than the guidelines, more subjective and concerned with psychology (perhaps even psychological warfare) than a rational, balance-sheet type of analysis. But don't underestimate them. Negotiating is a complex process that draws on all your skills, interpersonal as well as analytic.

For starters, you must prepare yourself for the specific negotiation at stake. Just like a good attorney researches his or her case, looking for precedents, so does a good negotiator. You want to know all you can about the person who will be sitting across the table: his or her personality, hobbies, pet peeves, special pleasures. A gentleman sitting beside me on a flight to California provided me with this gem: "It's not what you know, and it's not who you know, it's what you know about who you know that really counts." Good research takes time, sometimes days. Don't be afraid of the extra hours of work. Treat this as an investment that will pay dividends at the end of a successful negotiation.

A few years ago I was hired to negotiate a labor contract for a firm in upstate New York. As I was preparing myself, I learned by chance from one plant manager that he didn't think the union's business agent, who would be sitting across from me at the bargaining table, had read the union's bylaws in years. Needless to say, I hurriedly obtained a copy for myself and greedily studied it. I found a gem. At the appropriate moment in the bargaining, I threw out our offer, it was decidedly lowball, but I made it clear that we weren't going to budge. My opponent grew furious and announced he would take the offer to the membership. "Fine," I said. They overwhelmingly rejected it, as I presumed they would. He then called for a strike vote. I gambled that the union would reject going on strike and seek to prolong the bargaining process. Again, events turned out that way; there weren't enough votes to go on strike. Then I zeroed in for the kill, since in my arsenal I had the ultimate weapon—the rules of the union itself—which this agent had ignored. Under the bylaws, if a strike vote failed, the union was obliged to immediately ratify the contract offer on the table. I was astounded that the agent didn't know that—but he didn't. Meanwhile my client profited from very favorable terms during the life of that contract.

As the negotiation unfolds, you will be confronted with a fluid, sometimes confusing jumble of interaction. Few serious negotiations proceed in a straightforward, logical manner from point A to point B to point C. Instead, they jump around like the schematic diagram of a computer. Just like a computer, however, you need to be inputting all this assorted data into separate files so that at the right moment you can synthesize the various elements into the deal that you want.

One of the "files" should be titled "Specific Negotiable Items." Aside from those you define as part of your goals, other negotiable options will emerge during the course of your discussions. Another file should be "Opponent's Goals." You may be surprised to discover what is really at stake for the other side, but don't let on that you know until the right moment. What does your opponent need in order to walk away from the table feeling successful? You can find this out either by simply asking him or by getting him to prepare a document such as a lease, a loan agreement, or a letter of intent. You can use indirect methods such as reviewing other contracts he has negotiated (by contacting previous clients or opponents). You can even call him, disguising your voice and representing that you are interested in a product or service he offers.

Here's how I applied these principles in my first paid negotiating experience. It occurred when my basement flooded because of a faulty valve. At stake was a reasonably significant insurance claim. I realized rather quickly that the adjuster's goal was to delay so I would settle at a low price. I had two settlement options: accept payment equal to the original purchase price of each object less depreciation (which was negotiable) or obtain replacement of all the ruined objects (regardless of the current price). I decided that my goal was to obtain the maximum cash possible without having to replace each item. But I pretended that I wanted all the objects replaced, requiring a time-consuming inventory of soggy items, one by one, just to extend the bargaining process and also to let the adjuster think that his strategy of stalling was working. Then, finally, in supposed exasperation over the delays, I agreed to settle for cash, thus accomplishing my specific tactical objective, which was to negotiate the slightest possible depreciation and therefore set the highest amount for each item.

There's one final aspect of the well-stocked arsenal that I've left for last but which a successful negotiator does first. Include the word "relationship" in your first sentence addressed to your opponent. This gives you a tactical edge because it clearly establishes that you expect to continue doing business with him for a long time. Implant in his or her mind the possibility of a longer arrangement than simply this one-shot deal. As long as he thinks there will be a next time, he is less likely to bargain quite as aggressively as he might otherwise. But for you, negotiate each item down to the last dollar, because there is no time except the present!

As you roll out your arsenal and unfold your tactics, your opponent will not always know your negotiating direction.

Don't worry as long as *you* know—that's all that matters. From the opening moment, when you wedge the word relationship and the promise of future deals into the conversation, to the final payment of the last dollar, you must be committed to executing your game plan.

THE WINNING GAME PLAN

It is the winning game plan that gives you the negotiating edge, every time. In developing such a plan, you must be unconventional in both thought and action. As we saw with the labor union and the hotel negotiations, by taking an unexpected tack I was able to flank the opposition and secure a victory. You want to look at how to achieve your goals by using lateral thinking, approaching a problem from the side rather than straight-on, looking for new questions to ask rather than resorting to the same old answers, in which your opponent may be well versed. Always be looking for the new wrinkle, the unexpected inroad. Then have the courage to bring your game plan to the bargaining table—even if your opponent thinks you're nuts.

For each financial situation—negotiating for a loan, or a lease for an apartment, or better compensation, or selling a house—you must develop a different game plan. Your winning plan must include three essential components:

• *Goals.* You must establish a clear-cut overall goal and subgoals for each negotiable option. For example, if you are negotiating a loan, your overall goal is to borrow the most dollars at the least cost with minimum loss in financial flexibility. Your subgoals may include reducing the cost of the loan by lowering the interest cost and most of the other nickel-and-dime costs such as loan origination fees, discount points, and appraisal fees.

• *Options.* You must identify all the options and terms that you want to negotiate, including those you may add or withdraw during the negotiations.

• *Strategies.* You must develop an overall strategy to achieve your goals, as well as separate strategies tailored to each option. Each strategy will spell out the order you plan to negotiate each item, possible trade-offs of one option for another, and your minimum acceptable terms.

Developing a game plan, however, is not the same thing as pulling it off. The world is full of dreamers who can create spectacular strategies on a tablet of yellow legal paper but fold up under the pressure of face-to-face confrontation and lack the nerve to implement what they have conceived. Don't fall into that trap. The paper plan puts you at the base of the mountain; executing your winning game plan gets you to the top, where the financial treasures await you!

3

NEGOTIATING
FOR A LOAN

THE TROUBLE WITH most of us is that we mistakenly assume that banks write the rules, since they have all the money. Wrong! There is no situation better suited to tough, creative negotiating than when you're asking for a loan. It is the rare person, however, who dares to even disagree with a lender, let alone engage in serious negotiation. Most of us approach a banker with a humble trepidation that quickly renders us docile and passive. But that's absolutely the incorrect attitude. Remember: *Whenever money is at stake you can (and must) negotiate.* The more money at stake, the more reason to fight for your self-interest. Bankers expect the big boys to bargain hard over the terms of a loan. There's no reason why the rest of us shouldn't do the same.

Bankers and other lenders are just like any other merchant with a product to move. Forget the fancy trappings, the marble floors, the three-piece suits, the aura of impeccable respectability. These are just stage sets, props and costumes for the "theater" of finance. The drama itself is all about the buying and selling of money. That, after all, is what bankers do—they *buy* money (from the public in the form of deposits, or from the government, or from other financial institutions) and they *sell* it in the form of loans. Without a market, they're out of business just like any other merchant.

You need to keep this in mind as you prepare to apply for a loan. You are going to ask for money, not as a poor relative coming hat in hand to a rich uncle, but as a fellow financier who intends to pay for the privilege. And since you're paying your own way, you have the right and the opportunity to negotiate the terms. Nobody is going to tell you this. Bankers like the way the game is played, with all the advantages on their side. But you don't have to abide by their rules unless you want to be like an orange, which is how I think of most borrowers, who are having the juice squeezed out of them.

Few people understand this better than Ted Turner. He is brash, immodest, and unconventional. He has succeeded in borrowing enough money from enough sources to rank him, as he is fond of noting, among the biggest debtors in the history of mankind. Turner appreciates that bankers need to lend money, the more the better. He has established himself as a megaborrower, which lately was evidenced in his billion-dollar purchase of Metro-Goldwyn-Mayer. In this case he was after an inventory of movies to show on his cable television network, and he wagered heavily that the revenues from these movies ultimately would dwarf the expense of acquiring them. Time will tell. It is already evident, however, that Turner is a master of the principles of financial negotiation. He understands that one of the

54

keys to financial success is using the power of financial institutions to your own advantage by dealing with them on your own terms.

It isn't just the world-class players who can do this. An acquaintance of mine, Sue Laverty, also knows how to negotiate with bankers in terms they understand and respect. Sue is your average middle-class woman, a single mother who has been on her own for nearly a decade. A while ago she bought a new car and went to her bank for an auto loan. This is the same bank where she has a savings account, checking account, and periodically buys certificates of deposit to save for her children's college education. The bank was only too happy to make the loan, knowing her to be a reliable person of worthy credit, and they did so— at an annual rate of 10%. But before the arrangement was finalized and the papers signed, she learned that another bank across town was offering comparable loans at 8%. "Negotiate!" She was a little nervous; she had never before bargained with a bank and wasn't sure she could do it. Nevertheless, she went back to her banker, made it clear in a polite but forceful way that she knew of the alternative rate across town, and suggested that she, as a loyal customer, deserved the same consideration. She made it equally clear, in an equally polite and subtle way, that she was prepared at that moment to switch her accounts across town if she were refused. It took a little while. The loan officer had to consult the manager, and the manager in turn had to consult his boss at headquarters, but in the end her patience and determination were rewarded. Her bank matched the competition.

KNOW YOUR LENDER

For starters, you have to assess the priorities of your lender. I operate from the premise that every lender appraises your finances differently; every lender has his own special criteria that influence his decision to recommend or reject a loan. You need to figure out what makes him tick. Is he aggressive and daring? Is his institution? Or is it just the opposite: timid personality and ultraconservative institution? What does his institution require in order to make a loan? You may have to shop around for a banker and a bank that fit your needs, but don't regard this process as a nuisance or a waste of time. Rather, it is an investment, well worth any inconvenience.

You can find out how a potential lender will size up your financial situation by having someone else visit him with the same proposal and similar financial information to support the loan. The objective: to see what is the best deal he can negotiate. Of course, he won't have the same negotiating skills, but this will tell you that you can do even better. However, *don't* allow him to sign any documents such as a loan application—this constitutes misrepresentation. It is not necessarily the terms which your friend gets that are important, it's the process—specifically, the exact forms the lender uses to process and analyze your loan. Or you can go to another branch of the same bank and do the same thing. Be careful not to leave any information. Say "I'll bring it back if I'm interested in pursuing the matter." This is to prevent the possibility of an officer from another branch recognizing the information if a bank has several branches and operates with a joint loan committee. You can always take the direct approach and just ask the lender for the documents—its loan-disclosure form, its loan-analysis sheet, and the document it uses to analyze the profitability of its relationship with a borrower. I did and was successful with many banks including Citibank and Marine Midland, two of the largest. Sometimes I am successful; other times I have to go into the trenches and dig for it. If your efforts to get the information directly are fruitless, you can gather the information (such as a lender's cost of funds and profits) piecemeal from a lender's submissions to federal and state banking regulators. Or, if it's a public corporation, you can obtain its submissions to the Securities and Exchange Commission or its annual report. You can write or visit the local office of state or federal banking agencies to obtain this data. The information is important, is readily available, and with a little footwork you can obtain it.

You'll need to know the rules your lender plays by. The most important document you can secure is the profitability analysis form, which will tell you the value of your deposits to the bank and the profit the lender makes on your loan. Added together, the two tell you the profitability of your relationship to the lender. Once you know the profit a lender generates from your relationship, you can negotiate to whittle it down to meet your goals.

Here is how to calculate the profitability of your relationship to a lender. Let's assume that you want to borrow $56,000 for a three-year period. The repayment schedule leaves you with an average loan outstanding balance of $50,600 during the first year of the loan. In your research you determine that the particular lender you are considering can reinvest only 85% (it varies with state and federal banks) of your deposits (which you estimate will be $30,000). You also discover from its submission to the state banking authorities that its most recent month's cost of funds (the rate it pays to customers for deposits) was 7.25%. With this information and the Profitability Analysis Form in front of you, you can calculate the profitability of your relationship with the lender.

PROFITABILITY OF YOUR RELATIONSHIP TO A LENDER

Value of Your Account Balances to a Lender

FORMULA

$$\text{Value of Balances} = \text{Average account balance} \times \text{Percentage rate of account balance that can be reinvested} \times \text{Lender's cost of funds}$$

TO ILLUSTRATE

Average account balance = $30,000

Percentage rate of account balance that can be reinvested = 85%

Lender's cost of funds = 7.25%

Value of Balances = $30,000 × 0.85 × 0.0725 = $1848.75

Profitability of Your Loan

FORMULAS

$$\text{Gross Yield} = \frac{\text{Interest collected} + \text{fees}}{\text{Average loan outstanding}} \times 100$$

Net Spread = Gross yield − Lender's cost of funds

Loan Profitability = Net spread × Average loan outstanding

TO ILLUSTRATE

Interest collected = $ 5600

Fees $= \quad \$ \quad 200$

Average loan outstanding $= \quad \$50,600$

Lender's cost of funds $= \quad 7.25\%$

$$\text{Gross Yield} = \frac{5600 + 200}{50,000} \times 100 = 11.60\%$$

$$\text{Net Spread} = 11.60\% - 7.25\% = 4.35\%$$

$$\text{Loan Profitability} = 4.35\% \times \$50,000 = \$2175$$

Profitability of Your Relationship to the Lender

Profitability of your relationship to the lender		Value of your account balances		Profitability of your loan
$4023.75	=	$1848.75	+	$2175.00

As you can see, the lender earned $4023.75 profit by its deposit and lending relationship with you. How can you use this information to your advantage? You now know how much the lender's profit is on its relationship with you. You also know that he makes $1848.75 on the account balances you leave on deposit and $2175 profit on the loan. Tell a lender that you are aware of the value of your deposits and loan to him. Negotiate to reduce the interest cost on the loan and increase the interest rate you are earning on your deposits.

Take the time to do your homework such as gathering the information and filling in the lender's profitability analysis form. Avoid the temptation to accept the first loan you are offered if it isn't on your terms. When you find a lender who favorably perceives you and your financial situation, cherish him like a jewel—because that's what he is. Once you've found your lender, show him you care. I know how corny that sounds, but it works. Show him your interest in his institution by demonstrating that you took the time to fill out his forms. He'll probably be aghast at how you got hold of them (if he didn't give them to you). At the same time you are letting him know you are no dummy— you know the rules of the game—especially how he is going to analyze your loan request.

THERE IS ALWAYS AN EXCUSE

In a lending institution, as in any other corporation, there are front-line troops and the upper echelon to whom they report. In the beginning, as you establish yourself as a borrower, it will be the "mezzanine lender" who greets you, the fellow or woman in the nice but faceless office (the personnel change so often at this level that nobody leaves much of an impact on his or her surroundings). The mezzanine lender is probably more impressed with himself or herself and the stature of the institution than you are (although, of course, you don't want to show it). These are the kind of people who say no with great speed and immense delight. And their favorite reasons why? I've heard it so often I almost think these are the two holiest of holy psalms of the lending business, something employees are required to utter at least once a day or lose their jobs: "bank policy" and "the government regulators won't let me do this." Hogwash!

"Bank policy" is one of those great catchall phrases that can be used to explain away anything. Take the matter of collateral, for example. You never want to pledge collateral against a loan unless you are so backed up against the wall that you have absolutely no alternative (and even then you want to explore alternative possibilities). But if you listen to a mezzanine lender he'll condescendingly explain to you that pledging collateral is bank policy, no way around it. But this isn't a law written in stone. It is a practice that has been turned into tradition by the lender's attorney to protect his client's interest—nowhere is it said that a bank must take collateral before granting a loan. The same is true with interest rates. Nowhere is it written that a lender cannot give you a loan at a rate less than prime when it suits his purposes. Remember, it is the *profitability* of the total package that ultimately counts to the lender; the *specifics* of the way the loan is structured is only one element. So, if you know how the game is played, you can bend the rules to fit your own situation. Should a bank balk at granting a loan at the rates you propose, don't be intimidated, keep trying.

The same goes for supposed government regulations. When the lender invokes the sacrosanct name of The Government, it puts enormous power in his hands and corresponding fear in the heart of the borrower. Imagine the psychological impact of being able to threaten your negotiating adversary with the weight and wrath of the government should he fail to accept your terms! Don't buy into this mind game. The only thing the government cares about is that the loan is well documented (in terms of the right checks in the right boxes on the right forms) and that there will be, it is hoped, no missed payments. As long as these two conditions are met, the loan will not be rated by the government regulator as substandard. That's what all the talk about government regulations ultimately comes down to—is the documentation complete and the payback sufficient so that the loan is not in jeopardy and thus a potential threat to the bank's creditworthiness? So when a lender claims the terms you propose are contrary to government regulations, just smile politely and demonstrate to him that (a) your financial position can be amply documented and (b) you will have no problem servicing the loan on the basis of your cash flow.

Take, for example, the case of Jack Bernard. He is a prominent, wealthy businessman who is self-employed. He once applied for a loan, and although the lender knew Jack had sufficient cash flow to repay any loan (plus he had assets that could be liquidated if he ran into serious financial difficulties), the lender refused to approve it. Why? Because "rules are rules" and he needed to verify Jack's income. The only way that was possible was by examining his tax form. "I must see your 1040," the lender insisted (translation: he needed to be able to put a check next to the "income verified" box on the application forms). Jack, however, wasn't about to divulge the private information on his tax return, which revealed the sources of his income, his fees, his clients—very delicate stuff! What to do? At stake was a $100,000 loan. The lender wanted to grant it, Jack wanted to receive it. He came up with a brilliant face-saving compromise that solved the dilemma. As a verification of income, he proposed that the bank accept the annual deposits he made in his personal account as proof of income verification—this would in effect provide a record of the money he received in salary and from investments. It worked. The lender's no became a yes.

The tone and approach you take in your financial scenarios often can influence the lender to make decisions in your favor. As in that old song, you want to "accentuate the positive." If you are asking for a loan because of a temporary dip in your business, phrase your proposal (and your cash flow projections) in terms of "added funds" necessary to sustain anticipated growth. Cash shortfalls in pursuit of growth such as needing money to expand a store, or to develop a new market, are acceptable; emergency infusions of money to stave off disaster obviously aren't the kinds of loans lenders like to make. Increase the comfort level of your lender by packaging your requests within the framework of a growth plan.

YOUR GOAL

Borrowing money can be highly rewarding if you remember that there is only one goal: *Negotiate the maximum loan at the least cost with zero collateral and no constraints on your financial flexibility.*

YOUR STRATEGY

To win the negotiations with a lender, all you have to do is prove your ability to *service the debt.* First, seize control of the negotiating process quickly by presenting the lender

63

your most probable (not necessarily the most positive) cash flow projection. It should highlight the sources of your income and how you'll spend, save, and invest over the next three to five years. The Cash Flow Projection table that follows illustrates this. You can expand it even more by spelling out your expected sources of income and spending, saving and investing programs. The idea of course is to demonstrate that as you take on new debt, you can meet both the interest and repayment obligations.

The cash flow projection assumes that you have a cash surplus in all three years of the forecast. You have sufficient cash to meet your current needs, but not enough to cover additional debt service—interest expense and debt repayment—on any new loans. In year one, the projection demonstrates that if you borrow $25,000 and invest the total amount, after you combine the investment income ($4500) with the cash surplus before the loan ($9000) and then subtract the additional cash outlay ($10,000), you will have a cash surplus of $3500. Similarly, in years two and three you will have a cash surplus of $2640 and $7280 respectively. You will also have a cumulative cash surplus over the three-year period of $13,420. The cash flow projection demonstrates that in each of the three years you can support the additional debt service with your cash flow and still have a cash surplus remaining.

CASH FLOW PROJECTION

	Year 1	Year 2	Year 3
Cash In:			
Salary (after taxes)	$45,000	$52,000	$58,000

Bonus (after taxes)	5000	9000	12,000
Total	50,000	61,000	70,000
Cash Out:			
Life-style	28,000	45,000	45,000
(food, apartment,			
clothes, car)			
Savings	8000	7000	12,000
Investments	5000	–	1000
Total	41,000	52,000	58,000
Surplus	9000	9000	12,000

Amount of loan—$25,000
New investment—$25,000
Funds Available to Service Debt:

Surplus	$ 9000	$ 9000	$12,000
Income from investment	4500	3000	5000
Total	13,500	12,000	17,000
Less: Loan: Debt service:			
Interest	2000	1360	720
Repayment	8000	8000	9000
Total	10,000	9360	9720
Surplus after new loan	3500	2640	7280
Cumulative Surplus	3500	6140	13,420

Within this forecast you have included many of the dollar terms—amount of loan, repayment, and cost (the example shows interest only and zero fees) of the proposed loan for which you are applying. It demonstrates that you have excess cash after meeting the interest expense and repayment of the debt. These are the terms you anticipate you have the best chance of obtaining without too much objection from your lender—terms that are not necessarily the best you can get, but are very favorable for you. The forecast emphasizes your first objective: you can repay the debt. For instance, you don't want to get the lender side-tracked on a specific term, saying, "The interest rate is too low." Later on you can always refine your terms so they are more in your favor. And if the lender accepts the cash-flow figures as is, you are prepared to live with the deal. Next, as in the example, you must demonstrate to the lender, even before he asks the question, that you can handle this new debt. Now, if you were sitting on the other side of the table, as a lender, and somebody showed you a most-probable scenario, wouldn't you also want to see the worst-case scenario—you lose your job, the house burns down, your Great Dane requires triple bypass heart surgery? Don't wait for him to ask for it. Reach into your briefcase and pull it out. It should demonstrate to him that even if all these misfortunes occur, you can still repay the debt plus interest when it is due. Relieve your banker of his greatest fear—nonpayment of the loan—and you are three-quarters of the way to getting the loan on your terms.

What if you realize, after crunching the numbers, that you can't in fact repay the debt in a worst-case situation? All isn't lost. Just plan ahead! Anticipate the lender's questions and be prepared to respond that you have obtained insurance to cover all circumstances such as the house burning down, your being disabled, or your temporary inability to make the interest payments, and that you can provide third-party guarantees for the loan from employers, friends, or relatives.

Even if after doing this, a lender still insists that there is serious, legitimate doubt that you can repay him, and he insists on your putting up security and refuses to budge, then—but *only then,* and *only if you can't get better terms elsewhere*—assign the minimum collateral necessary to secure the note. And even at this point use the collateral for a useful purpose—to negotiate for a larger loan than your worst cash flow can support.

You might encounter a lender who says you either do business on his or her terms or not at all. In this case you must presuppose that you, the borrower, can demonstrate the ability to meet the debt service. Otherwise it doesn't work. It's not your fault—you've done everything right in negotiating for your loan, but the ending has turned out wrong. "Sorry, Charlie," the lender tells you. "No deal." Don't panic, persevere. Remember, there are two types of lenders in the world: those who are skillful and innovative, working out creative arrangements to serve everybody's interests, and those who plod along doing everything by the book. Unfortunately you have had the bad luck to be working with the second category. (You can guess what I think of them.) Forget them and go elsewhere.

If you feel that it's worth the effort trying to convince the lender otherwise, and decide not to accept his take-it-or-leave-it ultimatum, there are still options available to you. There are ways to get the lender to approve your loan on your terms—but you have to be smart and tough!

When you hit an apparent roadblock like this, don't vary

your strategy, but do change your tactics. Before, your objective was to execute your game plan according to *your* rules. Now you are still going to follow your game plan, but according to the *lender's* rules. Sound confusing? It really isn't. It just means that the negotiating game takes a new twist.

You'll have to find ways for the lender to depart from normal operating practices. Let's say you are applying for a $100,000 loan. The banker isn't entirely comfortable with the terms you have proposed. Why should he depart from his bank's traditional practices? As long as he continues to follow them, his tenure is reasonably certain. And here you come along with some crazy notions. But he is intrigued enough to listen. He is ambitious enough to wonder whether there might be some new opportunity here. But how do you assuage his fears and provide him with a rationale for approving your loan? Give him an opportunity to make more profit, even if it is minimal. Agree to pay a small amount, say a half-point fee, to guarantee you an extra $50,000 contingency loan should it ever be needed. The additional cost is marginal to you, probably around $250, and it is tax deductible. You get an extra fifty-thousand-dollar loan, and the fee will look good on the lender's book, justifying to him the value of your business—on your terms!

YOUR OPTIONS

Once you identify all your negotiable options, you will realize you have considerable flexibility in structuring the terms of the loan to achieve your goals. The four most important options to consider when negotiating a loan are:

amount of the loan
interest rate
duration
collateral

AMOUNT OF THE LOAN

Borrowing money is really a very simple proposition. The borrower determines how much money he or she wants. The lender decides how much money the borrower is "worth" in repayment terms. As long as you can demonstrate your capacity to pay back what you borrow, along with the interest, you can keep getting more money. Negotiation comes in when you get down to persuading the lender how much money you are worthy of borrowing and on what terms.

Your cash flow projection is very important; it is the vehicle which will verify that you have the wherewithal to assume this additional debt.

How large a loan a borrower should request and a lender should grant is rarely a clear, fixed figure. You can often get more than you need—the question is whether it is in your interest to do so. There are a few fixed, inviolable rules about either borrowing or lending, and even experts usually can't agree on the maximum financing ability of an individual or an organization. You almost always have room to negotiate. The difference between the amount you *could* borrow and the amount you *should* borrow defines the boundaries of your negotiation. It serves to define the "financial turf" over which you will be negotiating.

INTEREST RATE

Try to negotiate the lowest rate of interest. To do this effectively, it is important to understand how a lender generates profit on your loan. As I mentioned, a lender's profit includes the interest and assorted fees. A lender also makes money by investing the balances you leave on deposit in various checking and savings accounts. These balances have considerable value to the lender since they can be invested elsewhere, earning multiple returns.

A lending institution will try to charge you as much as it feels the market will bear. It determines profitability by calculating the spread between the price it pays for funds and the total rate of return (or yield) it can obtain by making a loan (interest rate plus assorted nickel-and-dime fees for loan origination, discount points, and appraisals). To this projected spread, the lender usually tacks on additional interest intended to protect itself from default; this added factor is the price the borrower is paying as a possible credit risk.

.

WHAT A LENDER CONSIDERS IN DETERMINING THE INTEREST RATE

investment returns to shareholders
administrative expenses
cost of money
value of borrower's balances
perceived credit risk
whatever interest rate the market will bear

The interest rates and the fees you pay to the lender are negotiable. Lots of people don't think that's true, but they are the same ones who never even dare test the waters to find out. Once you know the lender's cost and profit figures, as illustrated in the Profitability of Your Relationship to a Lender table, you can whittle down the basic interest rate to the lender's lowest acceptable one (which you determined from calculating the lender's anticipated profitability on your relationship). Do this by demonstrating that although the market may be willing to bear one rate, you know that there is surplus profit margin built into that rate and you expect some concessions. You also know that the lender has built some "insurance" into the rate to protect against default. Prove to the lender such insurance is not necessary since you are a superior credit risk. In this case you expect corresponding rate concessions. Finally, as you continue to negotiate, make it clear that your willingness to keep funds on deposit at the bank (the "indirect way" the lender generates profit) will be contingent on the interest rate you are given.

71

DURATION

Here you want the longest term, recognizing of course, that the longer the term the greater the total interest cost. However, you could always pay it back earlier if you so desire. The term has to be long enough to enable you to achieve your goals and repay the debt.

COLLATERAL

Collateral is probably going to be your biggest stumbling block. The mezzanine lenders are going to start out demanding that you put up an asset to secure your loan. Remember, your goal is to borrow the funds *unsecured* so that if you do hit some tough sledding and are unable to repay the loan, you still have the asset free and clear, and, therefore, flexibility. If you put up the asset as collateral and then default, you lose it—plain and simple. However, with an unsecured loan there are only two things that a lender can do in the face of default: reschedule the loan, working out a new arrangement for you to repay it; or take you to court, get a judgment of nonpayment, and then, under the authority of the judge, work out a repayment schedule.

When you borrow money you should never pledge assets as collateral with which to secure the loan; instead you should justify its repayment with future cash flow. I repeat: under only the most dire of circumstances do you want to get trapped into having to pledge collateral.

If you agree to provide collateral for a loan, you are

buying into one of the most preposterous of the myths perpetrated by lenders: that the value of collateral is somehow related to the amount of the loan.

Lenders like to have you believe they have a proven formula that relates the value of an asset to the amount of money a borrower can obtain toward acquiring that asset. They claim that the value of the asset is its perceived liquid value on the auction block. Then they add injury to insult by lending you money only up to a certain percentage of the appraised value of the asset.

What does this mean to you? First, you are forced to come up with a down payment that is the difference between the purchase price of an asset and the amount of the loan provided by the lender. This depletes your savings. Secondly, you have reduced rather than enhanced your financial leverage; you have tied up an asset that is worth, let us say, $125,000, in return for a loan of only $100,000. Borrowers and even lenders have begun to realize the error in keeping equity idle (in this case $25,000): tied up instead of being invested in income-generating opportunities. This accounts for the rapid growth in equity loans, which are really second mortgages, and, like the first mortgage, must be repaid when the house is sold (unless the loan is assumed by the buyer). Skilled financial negotiators do just the opposite—they parlay a little bit of asset to acquire a lot of cash with which they acquire more assets.

So where do you begin? *For starters, drop the term "mortgage" from your vocabulary.* Most of us think that's the only way to acquire a house or condominium. Remember, mortgage means a loan backed up by an asset, by collateral. When you provide collateral to secure a loan, you may increase the cost of the loan and reduce the flexibility of your investment. You can't sell the asset without repaying the loan, which might not necessarily be in your best interest. Worst of all, you have locked yourself into a pre-existent loan formula. This limits the amount of the loan to a proportion of the collateral and thus eliminates your ability to negotiate.

Instead, ask for a *loan* rather than a mortgage. Persuade the lender to make the loan by demonstrating that you can service it and pay it off on the basis of your cash flow. Your cash flow forecast must demonstrate that you have a surplus after paying the interest expense and meeting the repayment schedule. This is how third-world countries borrow money from American banks and how Fortune 500 companies do business. And you should too!

Even if you pledge an asset as security, and the asset is more valuable than the loan itself, you risk losing everything. I've seen it happen. Here's how. Say you borrow $30,000 and pledge collateral worth $40,000. When the bank takes possession of the collateral, it will sell off the asset as quickly and advantageously as possible. Because of a quick sale, the bank may realize considerably less than the asset's true value; or alternatively, it may structure a sale to a privileged buyer, maybe even itself in another corporate guise, at a price below the asset's market value.

What if the lender says "no way" whenever you try to structure an uncollateralized loan? Well, my best advice would be for you to politely say goodbye and walk out the door. You need a lender who understands cash flow. If yours doesn't, find another one.

Cash flow enables you to repay your debts—*if you don't*

have sufficient cash flow, you shouldn't borrow. And if you have a lender who doesn't fully appreciate the significance of your cash flow, you shouldn't be doing business with him. Find one who does—they are out there.

Here's an example of what is possible when you understand cash flow. In 1980, during the depth of a real-estate recession in Ohio, my buddy Paul wanted to sell his home. In spite of the slump, I encouraged him to set a fair market price, say $400,000. A buyer surfaced, willing to pay the price. If the new buyer had gone the traditional route, seeking a new mortgage, refinancing the existing mortgage of $140,000 (which Paul got before he met me), or getting the buyer to obtain a second mortgage, a banker would have lent the buyer 80% of the appraised value of the house, keeping the other 20% as "excess collateral." The buyer would have been short $80,000. I convinced Paul to finance part of the difference himself, on the basis of the buyer's cash flow. I found a bank that lent the buyer sufficient cash for a sizable down payment ($180,000) payable to Paul (keeping the first mortgage of $140,000 intact and adding a second mortgage for $180,000 for a total of $320,000) and then we arrived at a schedule for him to repay the difference ($80,000) to Paul at regular intervals. The buyer was able to buy the house with zero cash of his own and 100% financing. By using his cash flow to enhance his borrowing power, he was able to purchase a more expensive home. And Paul was able to sell his house at a high price.

Once the principles of the lending game regarding collateral are understood, they can be applied to a wide variety of situations and institutions. I once represented a client in

a deal with a U.S. government agency. He was a manufacturer who wanted a government loan to expand his
plant. Seated across from us at the negotiating table were
two prototypical stone-faced bureaucrats. They began the
proceedings by informing us that they couldn't even consider giving my client a loan without a personal guarantee
and the pledging of his assets (personal as well as business)
against possible default. Unfortunately, this deal was critical
to my client; the agency was his lender of last resort at the
time. Nevertheless, I wasn't about to let him enter into that
kind of arrangement. I knew that these men, with their
austere, take-it-or-leave-it style, actually had considerable
discretionary power in determining the terms of a loan. I
also knew that there were precedents in which comparable
agency loans had been obtained without pledging personal
collateral. I asked them if there had ever been cases in
which the guarantee and collateral requirement had been
waived. They laughed at what they took to be a naive
question. Okay, I went on, if I could demonstrate that there
were such instances, and that the particulars were similar
to those of my client, would they reconsider the terms?
They agreed. I showed them chapter and verse. They were
appropriately humbled, and to their credit they honored
their promise. Moral: If you dare to negotiate what seems
like the unnegotiable, you will often be surprised at what
happens. In this instance, by knowing that collateral and
personal guarantees were negotiable, and that I was dealing
with people who could make discretionary decisions, my
client and I took on the most conservative of lenders and
got a loan on our terms.

76

OTHER NEGOTIABLE OPTIONS

Once you have completed negotiating the four key items—amount of the loan, interest rate, duration, and collateral—you should focus on the other important items for which you have developed an individual strategy. These would include things such as *other fees* that would increase the cost of the loan and could add up to more than the interest. For example:

> origination fees
> discount points
> appraisal fees
> attorney's fees
> mortgage-insurance premium
> credit life-insurance premium

Origination fees. These are usually justified to a borrower as the cost of preparing the loan documents to "originate" the loan. Rubbish. A lender socks you with this so he can increase the yield rate on his money. He might, for example, try to charge you 10% interest plus a 2% origination fee, thereby increasing the yield rate from 10% (interest only) to 10.2% over a ten-year period.

Or he will offer you the "opportunity" of a lower interest rate, say 9.5% instead of 10%, if you just pay a 2% origination fee. It looks tempting at first, but remember: (1) the 2% is paid up front *out of the proceeds of the loan,* so you lose money right away, and (2) the annual percentage rate to the borrower (the yield rate to the lender) will increase.

The latter can add up, especially if you plan to repay the loan after only a few years, for the origination fee will increase the yield rate to 10.5% each year (9.5% interest plus 1% origination fee for each of two years).

Do not pay loan origination fees unless forced to. Consider paying them only if (1) they are accompanied by a lower interest rate, (2) you don't need the additional loan proceeds, or (3) it is a long-term—say, fifteen-year—loan. Its impact is minimal.

Your strategy: Convince the lender that the interest rate is the only charge you are going to pay. Explain that you are quite aware of how he calculates the profitability of the loan, that there is sufficient profit already built into the interest rate he is charging you. If he wants additional yield, he can get it from your deposit balances if you have them in the bank. They may not amount to very much (unbeknownst to the lender at the time the deal is made), since you will not commit to any specific amount or percentage of the loan.

Discount points. Each percentage point that a loan is discounted reduces its proceeds to a borrower. A discount point of 3% means that for a $100,000 loan, for example, a borrower will receive $97,000: the lender keeps the rest. Besides getting less money, the annual percentage rate that a borrower pays also increases. If the interest rate is 10%, the interest expense would be calculated on the $100,000 amount—even though the borrower received only $97,000! At 10%, the interest cost the first year would be $10,000 (10% of $100,000) while the yield rate to the lender would be 10.3% ($10,000 interest for loan proceeds of only $97,000),

78

an increase in the annual percentage rate to you of .3%.

Your goal: Get the lender to eliminate the discount points. Your strategy: Tell him, "I need the $100,000—otherwise why would I ask for it?" Don't accept the reply, "In that case I'll lend you $3000 more," or your cost of interest will increase; you'll pay interest on $103,000. Instead, you should do the same as you did to eliminate the loan origination fee, by pointing out the additional yield he can get from your deposit balances which, of course, may not to amount to very much (again unbeknownst to the lender at the time the deal is made), since here too, you will not commit to any specific amount or percentage of the loan.

Appraisal fees. This is one of those additional costs (inspection fees are another—you pay the cost of an on-site, eyeball inspection of the asset) that you invite when you agree to put up collateral. A lender may not accept your valuation of the asset and will have an appraiser estimate it. (The lender, of course, will try to get you to pay the cost of the appraiser.)

Your goal: Don't provide collateral in the first place. If you absolutely have to, in order to get the loan to buy, say, a new home, let the builder pay the appraisal fee since he is the one who is questioning your valuation of the asset. Your strategy: Tell the lender you have no intention of paying the appraisal fee, period. If that doesn't work, at least try to negotiate a lower fee.

Attorneys' fees. Have your attorney review your loan documents before signing them, but don't let the lender talk you into paying legal fees to *his* attorney for drawing up the agreement and protecting the lender. Legal fees can sometimes exceed the cost of the loan! Most lenders keep attorneys on a retainer basis anyway—all they want is to get you to help them recoup their legal expenses.

Your goal: Pay only *your* legal fees. Let the bank pay its own. Make this clear as soon as you can. If the lender won't buy this, ask him to get you quotations from three law firms that have prepared similar loan documents. After selecting the lowest-cost firm, agree to pay *only* for the specific phrases that pertain to your loan and have never been used in any previous loan. The cost will be minimal, since the firm has probably included these phrases in other agreements, and it has all the other parts of the agreement in its word processor.

Mortgage-insurance premium. Here, a lender not only wants collateral to secure the loan, he also wants you to buy insurance to pay it off should you die or (depending on the specifics of the policy) otherwise be unable to do so. This is expensive insurance for two reasons: (1) the face value of the coverage decreases as the amount of the loan declines—you pay the same premium whether the amount of the loan is $100,000 or $15,000—and, (2) the premium is usually inflated to provide the lender with a sales commission!

Your goal: Don't agree to purchase mortgage insurance. When is enough, enough? Not only does the lender have your cash flow to back up the loan, he also has collateral—and now he wants insurance as well!

Your strategy: You won't get into this position if you succeed in justifying the loan *on the basis of your cash flow.* If you don't succeed, and agree to put up collateral, ask whether the lender already has an insurance policy to cover possible default on the loan. If he does, why should *you* have to pay the premium? If he doesn't, ask whether he intends to sell the loan to another party. It is usual for a lender to merely close on a loan and then sell it, all the while collecting your interest and debt repayments and for a fee forwarding them to the holder of your note. If he plans to sell the loan, ask whether the mortgage insurance is part of the package and really necessary; in most cases it is not, and therefore you shouldn't pay the premium.

Credit life-insurance premium. On most standard loan documents there is a section devoted to credit life-insurance options with the phrase, "You are not obligated to purchase credit life-insurance." So don't. In an unsecured loan, it is your cash flow that supports the debt service. Why add to the cost of the loan by agreeing to pay an insurance premium?

Your goal: Don't pay the premium. If the lender wants to take out insurance on the loan, let him pay.

Your strategy: Don't even consider this insurance if a lender brings it up. Tell him it's not necessary—your cash flow is sufficient to meet the interest expense and debt repayment. However, remember that an insurance policy is better than providing collateral; all you do is pay the premium—you can't lose the asset. So if you have run out of options (unusual to say the least) and you agree to provide an insurance policy to secure an unsecured loan, consider taking out a term (risk-only) policy from another source; it is usually much cheaper.

Now it's time to consider the other negotiable items that may have a significant impact on your financial flexibility. The four most important ones are:

prepayment penalties
personal guarantees
no additional debt
no-assignment-of-assets pledge

Prepayment penalties. Your financial flexibility is severely limited if you are not allowed to repay a loan before it falls due. A lender especially likes to include a prepayment penalty when interest rates are high, thus locking in a borrower for a specific number of years and guaranteeing himself a high rate of return for those years. The purpose of the penalty is to discourage the borrower from refinancing when interest rates decline or paying off the loan early if the interest burden is too heavy. If a borrower decides to repay the loan before it is due, the penalty, usually a percentage of the loan, say 10%, has to be paid in addition to the outstanding portion of the loan. This can amount to a lot of money.

Your goal: Avoid prepayment penalties. They only reduce your financial flexibility, particularly your right to refinance to get the best deal in the future.

Your strategy: Emphasize your total relationship with a lender. Ask him, "How can you be helping me grow financially, and therefore retain income as deposits, if you limit my flexibility? You are restricting my right to make profits by locking me in to more costly financing." Make the lender decide: higher interest rates or receive the penalty, no loan and potentially lower deposits.

Personal guarantees. This option arises when you borrow on behalf of a business. *You should never—and I repeat, never—personally guarantee a business loan.* If your company goes down the tubes and can't repay the debt, you have to make up the shortfall even if you have to use up your cash reserves or sell your house and all your personal assets to do it. Time and again I've heard people tell me, "It can't ever happen to me; my business is a sure thing!" Well, it happens. Financing a business should be based on its cash flow, no different from justifying a loan on the merits of your personal cash flow. If you introduce cross-collateralization (using personal assets to secure a corporate loan or vice versa) or cross-signatures (personally signing for a corporation), you are dramatically increasing the risk if you default on the loan.

A lender will justify his need for a personal guarantee as a means of ensuring that you won't run away if the firm defaults. He will claim that he would need your help to continue to run the business if the bank decided not to foreclose and instead tried to turn the business around and help it repay the loan. Or, conversely, if it wanted to wrap up the business. That's just blarney intended to appeal to your ego, proclaiming "you are needed." Don't believe it. If a business loan goes bad, then you, personally, should be able to walk away free and clear from any obligations.

Your goal: Avoid a personal guarantee. I have never seen a lender decide not to grant a loan if all the other terms have been agreed on. *Always sign a business loan with your title beside your name,* thus making it clear you are signing only as an officer of a corporation and are not personally liable for any part of the loan.

Your strategy: Delay any discussion of personal guarantees until the last item to be discussed. Never introduce it yourself. Sometimes a lender won't even bring it up. He may point to a special line on the loan agreement for you to sign your name (without any title). *Don't do it.* If he says he won't give you the loan otherwise, then consider walking. Don't say to yourself, "I've come this far, I can't walk away now." That's exactly what your opponent wants you to do. However, before walking, ask him, "What good is my personal signature going to be? You already have my credibility on paper—I signed the document, didn't I?" And if he counters, "Well, we want your personal involvement too," say, "You have it. If that's not good enough, then you shouldn't be making me the loan in the first place. If you are prepared to cancel the loan, go ahead."

No additional debt. A lender would prefer that most of your loans be with him. His intent: to control the amount of debt that you incur, and to ensure that your cash flow is "reserved" to pay the interest and principal.

Your goal: To maintain your right to borrow as much as you can justify and repay.

Your strategy: Demonstrate to a lender, using your cash flow projection, that you have a surplus cash flow sufficient to repay any debt you might incur. Treat each new loan as a separate item, isolating the excess cash flow and demonstrating how that particular loan will be repaid, including the interest expense. Demonstrate this to a lender, using both your most-probable and worst-case cash flow scenarios.

No-assignment-of-assets pledge. Sometimes a lender will try to "camouflage" an unsecured loan by having you agree not to pledge those assets he would have liked to have as collateral, plus all other assets, for any loans whatsoever. If you do this, you are reducing your financial flexibility in

84

case you have to use those assets to secure a loan that you can't justify with your cash flow.

Your goal: Don't agree to such a pledge.

Your strategy: Demonstrate to the lender, using your cash flow projection, that you can cope with your debts. Use your most probable and worst-case cash flow scenarios. Don't mention that you would consider using collateral with another lender if he wouldn't otherwise give you a loan.

RED FLAGS

Okay, you've negotiated skillfully to get the loan you want on your terms. Nice going. But don't congratulate yourself too soon. You're not quite ready to pop the champagne. There is one last bridge that you have to cross— you still have to examine and sign a contract.

Be sure you're protected in the final agreement. Once you and the other side sign on the dotted line, the deed is done and the terms of the deal legally binding. So go over the language and the terms of the agreement very carefully. Avoid anything that restricts your financial flexibility.

Here are some red-flag phrases you need to be on guard against in the final document. They are traps. Beware of them!

Wage assignment. This stipulation empowers the lender to attach a portion of your wages if you default. (There is no need to describe how unpleasant this could be.)

Balloon. This is a large payment due on the loan at maturity. It can affect your principal and interest costs. Be

85

aware of the final balloon amount and make sure that you will be able to repay it when it comes due without having to resort to potentially costly refinancing.

Right of offset. This means that if you default, the lender can take funds directly from your checking or savings account to repay the debt.

Waive your rights under the bankruptcy law. This phrase means you give up any protection of assets provided under the bankruptcy laws.

Waive your rights to rescind the transaction during the three days following the transaction. Here you give up your right to void the agreement within three days of signing the documents.

Right to accelerate. This allows a lender to accelerate payment of the loan prior to its original maturity date for any specified reason, such as evidence that a borrower's credit situation has worsened.

Default without notice. This means that the lender can declare you in default and accelerate the repayment of the loan without notification. You will not be given adequate time to correct the causes of the default.

Lender can sell collateral before a judgment of default has been rendered. This means that if you are behind in repayment, the lender can sell the collateral to raise funds to repay the loan even before a judge rules that default really did occur. You could always obtain an injunction to stop the sale, but it is better to eliminate this clause from the agreement.

Lender may be the purchaser of all or any part of the collateral sold. This allows the lender to sell or buy the collateral

86

if you default. He can also charge you for all costs associated with the sale!

Default will occur if there is a change in "management" or "ownership." This is used when a loan is made for the purpose of starting or acquiring a business and is contingent upon the direction and/or ownership of that business remaining stable.

Now and hereafter. The collateral you provide as security for a loan, and any of the same assets you acquire in the future (even if you didn't make the loan to acquire the assets), will be used as security for the debt.

Default can occur for reasons other than nonpayment of principal and interest. This means that there are other conditions besides failure to repay that can trigger default.

The lender's attorney is your attorney-in-fact. This authorizes the lender's attorney to act on your behalf as well as that of the lender. You are agreeing to release the attorney from any future charges of conflict of interest.

Lender has all the rights and remedies available to a secured party. This is a dangerously general stipulation that gives the lender all kinds of leeway even if you don't default on the loan.

Borrower agrees not to incur any additional debt. This stipulates that you will not make any more loans while you have an outstanding loan with the lender. As mentioned, this clearly limits your subsequent financial flexibility.

Collateral that is not security with this lender can't be used as security elsewhere. This restricts your ability to borrow with any of your assets as collateral.

Notwithstanding the foregoing. This jawbreaker pertains

to the last paragraph of an agreement whereby all the terms agreed to preceding this phrase could be negated and only those following it constitute binding parts of the agreement.

Diplomacy is usually part of the negotiating process; you and a skillful banker both appreciate the value of being gracious and accommodating without surrendering your points of view. As such, minor corrections to an agreement at a closing are standard practice. Don't let these small annoyances develop into major problems. However, there may come a time when you have to play hardball with a banker, especially when the document doesn't reflect his or her commitment. Laura and Phil Berman, former neighbors of mine, had signed a contract to buy a house and negotiated a deal according to the game plan we had worked out with a savings and loan association. The Bermans received a disclosure statement from the S&L detailing the arrangement. At the closing session, however, there were a number of surprises—none of them pleasant for the Bermans. For starters, the interest rate was higher than on the agreement. The S&L wanted to establish an escrow account for taxes and insurance, contrary to what had been previously agreed. The closing costs included a loan origination fee and discount points that weren't on the loan disclosure statement. The Bermans were committed to closing on the house they were selling the same day. They were understandably upset. They telephoned me and I quickly arrived at the S&L, geared up for battle. In no uncertain terms I informed the lender that we knew we had the law on our side and that the negotiated items on the disclosure statement were the terms of the deal. Period. If the bank refused to finalize the loan according to the disclosure statement, we would sue it for breach of contract as well as for damages associated with the loss of the sale of my client's home. After a few phone calls the presiding loan officer agreed with our wisdom. The papers were signed.

HANGING TOUGH

Your lender can say no even after the deal has been structured and the loan granted. Remember, as Yogi Berra says, "It ain't over until it's over." Let's say you are in a situation in which you succeeded in borrowing funds unsecured by collateral with the understanding that you have been promised more funds. You may not have the commitment in writing (which you should have) but you have your lender's word (which is usually good). However, when you try to renew the existing note, your lender balks. He claims, perhaps, that your credit position has changed (untrue) or that bank policy has changed (who cares?). Either way you're in an exposed position—you don't have the money on hand to repay the debt—and you are justifiably outraged. What to do? *Play hardball.* File suit against the officers and directors of the lending institution, claiming duress, misrepresentation, breach of contract, conspiracy, violations of contractual obligation, and anything else that carries with it the stinging rage of actionable insult. An advantage to this sort of attack is that it doesn't cost much, usually between $500 and $2000, and it is sure to get your lender's attention. (Be aware, however, that the lender can countersue, claiming you filed a frivolous suit. So think this out before you call an attorney and yell "sue.") The best thing about this type of action is that during the interim, as your case works its way through the judicial system, the lender will be enjoined from calling your note and you will have bought yourself some valuable time. You can drive your lender crazy, requiring him to spend endless hours gathering documents and answering questions, turning them over to yours and the public's eyes. And the adverse public relations that the lender gets is not usually welcome. Finally, if you eventually lose the case three or five years down the road, it may cost you only the amount you owe anyway; legal fees and court costs must be awarded by the judge, and the lender may end up paying them. So don't ever be afraid to get your lender's attention by threatening to kick him where it hurts. And remember, while the attorneys are doing their thing, the door is still open for a favorable negotiated settlement.

ETHICS

A word about the ethics of borrowing. As you flex your mental intellect and display your tenacity, you are walking a fine line. You are making commitments, presenting yourself as capable of following through on what you claim, asking the other side to trust your character and integrity. That's not something to play with lightly, much less disregard. You don't ever want to be accused of being unethical; of doing something illegal or misrepresenting yourself. You cross that line when you borrow money with the intention of defaulting. Nobody can ever accuse you of unethical conduct if you make it clear right from the start what your goal is: to negotiate a loan on your terms.

A WORTHWHILE EFFORT

One of the greatest satisfactions a negotiator can experience is the pleasure of getting your opponent to say yes. It can be done. You can do it. And when a lender gives you money on your terms, the pleasures of negotiating are doubly sweet, since it carries direct financial gain for you!

THE WINNING GAME PLAN: A SUMMARY

Financial Situation: You want to borrow money.

Your Goal: The biggest loan at the least cost, with zero collateral and no constraints on your financial flexibility.

Your Strategy: Seize control of the negotiating process quickly by presenting the lender your most probable (not necessarily the most positive) cash flow projection, which contains many of the dollar terms—amount of the loan, repayment terms, and cost of the proposed loan. Demonstrate that as you take on new debt, you can meet both the interest and repayment obligations. Show the lender a forecast based on a worst-case scenario that will also demonstrate that even if misfortunes occur, you can still repay, when due, the debt plus interest. Relieve your banker of his or her greatest fear: nonpayment.

Your Options: Negotiate the four options in the order presented and the others on the checklist according to your priorities.

Key Items

—Amount of loan
—Interest cost
—Duration
—Collateral

Other Negotiable Items

—Escrow account
—Notary fee
—Discount points
—Asset-appraisal fee
—Loan discount
—Lender's inspection fee
—Mortgage insurance
—Title abstract
—Title insurance
—Transfer fees

—Prepayment penalty
—Commitment—future loans
—No other debt
—Commitment fee
—Repayment schedule
—Fees—your attorney
—Fees—lender's attorney
—Loan assumption fee
—Loan origination fee

—Credit report
—Hazard-insurance premium
—Title search
—Government filings
—Property survey
—Credit life insurance
—Personal guarantee
—No assignment of assets

4

NEGOTIATING COMPENSATION PACKAGES

THERE ARE FEW things in your life more important to you than your job. It provides you with income, social status, insurance, paid vacations, retirement benefits, perhaps perks like an automobile or membership in a country club. Think about it! How much of what you are is your job? Yet I am amazed at how few people get all the salary, benefits, and perks they really could. Whatever your situation, whether you're changing jobs or staying where you are, you can get a better compensation package than you now imagine possible. You can get those goodies, providing, that is, you negotiate!

Be bold and daring is what I tell my clients when they are working out the terms of an employment relationship. There is a lot of margin built into any compensation package. If the company is paying you $100,000, they must figure you're worth twice that to them. Get your piece of that action. "Ask, and you've got a good chance to receive," is how I would rephrase a biblical homily in the context of job negotiations—"But if you *don't* ask, don't be disappointed by what you *don't* get."

I don't know why so many people get so shy when it comes to negotiating with an employer. Perhaps they consider it bad manners to toot their own horn. But if they don't, who will? Perhaps they are afraid that the boss will say no and they'll lose face or, worse, lose the job. I admit that it takes guts and initiative to ask for benefits your employer doesn't voluntarily offer, but if you don't think you're worth those extras, why should your boss? You intend to work hard for your boss, you are good and you know it. Don't be afraid to expect—and ask for—appropriate compensation for your labors and contribution!

One of the key mental attitudes in negotiating for salary and perks is recognizing that you are responsible for your own destiny. Losers complain, winners negotiate! The amount of money you have left in your pocket after you cash your paycheck and pay your taxes is the real payoff you are getting from your job. This puts aside such intangibles as satisfaction, which won't do you much good when you're in the check-out line at the grocery store. If you are unhappy with your salary and benefits, you have two choices. One is to "keep on keeping on" as you're doing, allow others to make the critical decisions affecting your financial well-being, and reconcile yourself to a lesser life-style than you know you deserve. The second is to take control of your situation, decide what you're worth and what you want—and negotiate to make it happen.

THE NEW REALITY

If you decide to negotiate, you must fully understand the new corporate attitudes toward employees and compensation. The economic fluctuations of the last six years have taught executives that there is a new way of doing business in America. Irving S. Shapiro, the retired Chairman of Du Pont, says, "Two recessions almost back-to-back have educated all of industry to the fact that it has to operate on a different basis." *Business Week*'s headline on its front cover, November 28, 1983, read, AMERICAN BUSINESS IS UNDERGOING ITS FIRST REDIRECTION IN 50 YEARS. Roger B. Smith, Chairman of General Motors, has called the GM reorganization "a return to basics."

Does this mean that as an employee you have less negotiating power? No! It just means you have to be even more determined and skillful in negotiating salary and perks. Also, it means that you have to be alert to the new opportunities offered by the strategies of firms that are in either survival or growth postures.

If you interview with a firm that is in a survival mode, you would think at first blush that there would be no room for negotiating, that their policy would be to reduce "people costs." This is quite true. If you are trying to break into a firm that is growing fast, it will most likely be looking for new workers, suppliers, facilities, and financing, and there will be others competing for your job. But in either case, if you really have the skills that are needed, you can negotiate.

The potential for greater compensation does not, however, come without increased risks in the above two cases, so if you think the firm you are interviewing with might go under, or if you aren't willing to hitch a ride on a (possibly) rising corporate star, stay away from companies that are precarious or booming and approach more stable organizations.

PREPARING FOR THE INTERVIEW

Regardless of whether the company is steady and solid, barely surviving, or booming, you must be well prepared for the interview. I can't stress this enough. First you must have your facts—all you can learn about the company and its policies. If it's a public corporation, you should study the annual report and SEC submissions to determine what salary and fringe benefits are offered to the top executives. This information should be available from the stockholder or investor relations department. Call and ask them to send it to you. Better, if the company is close by, go and pick it up. This will let you see their offices. If they are reluctant to give it to you, tell them you are a potential investor. If you are still unsuccessful, ask a stockbroker to get it for you. The annual report will tell you about the firm's financial progress. Obtain the 10K (annual) and 10Q (quarterly) submissions to the SEC. It is in the 10K that you are most likely to find out about compensation to the firm's top officers. If the firm is a financial institution such as an insurance company or a bank, you can get this data from their submissions to either state or federal regulatory authorities.

If the firm is privately owned, you may not be able to

get exact figures on salaries and perks, but you can get useful approximations. Read the reports of similiar companies. Read the want ads in the local and national papers to determine the compensation packages being offered in comparable situations. Find out how other employers set their salary and fringe benefits.

Whether the firm is public or privately owned, there are other ways to find out compensation information. Go to your public library and look up Moody's, Standard and Poor's, and other books (for example, a regional manufacturing or service guide) that could tell you who owns the firm, who its directors and exectutives are, and even their pay. Read local or national magazines. Get copies of the in-house organs. Call the local branch or national headquarters of trade associations in the same industry as the firm, whether you know if the firm is a member or not, and see if they have employment and compensation data. Be selective, however—you don't want to get bogged down in mountains of information.

What you want to know is:

• What are your skills worth in the context of the company, the industry, and your locality? You must assess your worth in relation to others. You don't want to get locked in to your firm's current salary levels and basket of offerings.

• Does the firm determine salary levels for employees in terms of their specific performance and contribution or are there predetermined levels of compensation?

• Are compensation packages commensurate with responsibilities?

- If a job is billed as part of an esteemed management-training program, does salary reflect the importance the company attaches to the program? (If not, there may be reason to suspect that the "training" may lead nowhere.)
- Where is your predecessor in a specific position of interest to you going?
- How many people who have worked at this level are still with the company? How many have risen to higher positions? How do salaries increase at higher positions?

Why do all this research? Because the answers to these questions will help you determine the compensation package you intend to negotiate. Plus you want to make sure that the deal you negotiate puts you at the top of any job or grade classification. Why? Because this will make it easy for the company to promote you; you are avoiding a situation in which your advancement and compensation are in lockstep with others in your department or category.

A second crucial step in preparing for the interview is to create a résumé that is a marketing masterpiece. It should derive its merit not only from the things it tells about you, but from its structure and ability to focus the interviewer's attention on the credentials that you want to highlight. This calls for meticulous preparation and thoughtful presentation. The résumé must be self-explanatory (especially if you have to mail it in before you are granted an interview) and make a statement on your behalf as to your capability to excel in the position you are seeking, walking the reader in the direction of your strengths and away from any weaknesses. It must be factually correct, since verification is easy, but you should highlight only the most positive aspects.

MENTAL POSTURING

Picture it. You and the interviewer sitting eyeball to eyeball, both holding your future in your hands. Intimidating? Only if you let it be. You must not fail to recognize that you have the most leverage at the time you take a new job. Your prospective employer has a slot to fill. Why else would they be hiring? And you are the person they want to fill it. Why else would they be offering you a job?

You also have leverage if you are currently an employee of the firm. You can improve your situation at your present job without threatening to quit. However, when you are involved in a job-performance review, your strategy is a little different and a little more delicate. You know that it is not easy to walk away from a career. And the interviewer knows it too; he or she doesn't want to be responsible for giving you reason to leave. So you both have to be cautious. The interviewer may see the review only as confirmation of your ability to do your current job, but *you* should see it as an opportunity to negotiate for advancement and more money. So take the initiative and schedule the session slightly in advance of its traditional date, to give you a slight edge in the game. If asked why, answer, "To know where I stand in the firm." *Don't* suggest that you will consider looking elsewhere for a job if you are unhappy with the results of the review. That smacks of disloyalty—the unforgivable sin of corporate life, and is virtually guaranteed

103

to defeat your negotiation before you start. But the message will register with your superiors that something is afoot.

YOUR GOAL

Your primary goal when negotiating for compensation is to maximize your salary and fringe benefits after taxes and inflation.

Be taxwise—think compensation only "after taxes." To figure out the value of a perk, compute what it would cost you if you had to purchase it yourself with after-tax dollars. Say, for example, you were offered the use of a company car in lieu of money. The monthly note for the car is $250, insurance is $100, maintenance is $50; thus to support this car you would need $400 a month, or $4800 a year. You are in the 28% tax bracket. In order to net $400 a month after taxes, you would have to gross $555. So the $4800 automobile package is worth $6667 pretax dollars.

You must also consider the impact of inflation on such long-term fringe benefits as pension or profit-sharing plans and deferred-savings plans. You should negotiate the amount of the firm's contribution, the way the funds are invested, and your ability to access these funds. There is no use negotiating a deferred benefit such as a profit-sharing, pension, or deferred-savings plan when the earnings on the funds accumulate at less than the rate of inflation, since the money in the plan will have less value to you than if you took it out now, paid the taxes, and invested it yourself.

104

YOUR STRATEGY

The negotiating process began even before the interview, when you sent in your résumé for a new job by mail or asked to schedule your job-performance review earlier than usual. Keep this in mind when you walk in the door and shake hands with the interviewer.

Follow the same game plan when you're negotiating your annual review as you would if you were seeking a new job. Begin the interview by placing a current résumé, a marketing masterpiece, in front of the interviewer, even if you have been an employee for five years and he or she has your personnel file right on the desk. Direct his attention to point after point on your résumé in order to get him to acknowledge your self-evaluation. "Are you aware of the work I do at St. Jude's Hospital on the weekends?" Go even further, stating, "It was my idea to develop that prescription-drug management program." The more you get the interviewer to focus on specific points, the more you must be prepared to withstand the closest scrutiny, inviting questions such as, "What makes you successful at what you do?" and more questions, so that you can provide image-boosting answers to enhance your credibility. This is your time to toot your own horn and orchestrate the interviewer's attention, never losing sight of your goal. It is the carefully prepared résumé that allows you to accomplish your goals by getting the interviewer to follow *your* agenda and not his or hers.

Don't be bashful, overly aggressive, or impatient. Bide your time, continually demonstrating your indispensability to the firm, relying, if necessary, and taking credit if possible, on your leadership in a previous job well done or when you exploited an opportunity—even if your associates contributed as much as you did. If there is credit to be given, *you* take it! This is the time to draw long, deep breaths, take emotional account of yourself, leaving to the interviewer's perception the potential consequences of your deciding not to work for his or her firm. As the session continues to unfold, you should always suggest that you are eager to take on more responsibilities in order to further contribute to the growth of the company. Give the interviewer little choice except to offer you the job or a promotion.

After you have answered all the interviewer's questions, it is time to introduce the subject of money. Don't leave it to the end of the interview as an afterthought, as most people do—bring up the subject *early*. As with any financial negotiation, you need to determine quickly whether there is the basis for a deal. If there is none, why proceed? Once you mention money, the tone of the conversation is bound to change. The interviewer may not be prepared for this, he or she will wonder whether money is all that counts with you. That's okay, don't worry. Up to this point you were both engaged in a coy courtship dance; henceforth you have put him or her on notice that you are a serious, self-confident person. Equally important, you now have the mandate to begin selling hard, telling the interviewer why you, and only you, can do best this job and even more advanced ones.

Be warned, however, that most interviewers will try to stay away from early discussions of money. As soon as that touchy subject comes up, it will be more difficult to continue to induce the interviewer to follow your agenda instead of his. He will want to avoid the topic, recognizing that once you've decided that the basic compensation package is inadequate, you aren't going to be impressed with the office decor or the daily luncheon specials in the executive cafeteria. He will want to avoid the subject until the end, after he has sold you on the job. The more reluctant the interviewer is to talk about money, the more you want to stay with it and force the subject.

Always ask for more compensation—salary and fringe benefits—than the company traditionally would offer. This convinces them to take you seriously by letting them know you take yourself seriously. You will be sending a strong signal to the people in the company responsible for deciding your compensation package. Without ever having to say it in so many words, you will be letting them know they have a choice; give you damn near what you want or be prepared for you to leave at the first opportunity! Never be apologetic in making your demands, or thankful for what you're currently receiving—you earn what you get, you deserve more!

YOUR OPTIONS

Salary and fringe benefits constitute the principal parts of your compensation package. The key salary and fringe-benefits include three cash options and one fringe benefit, the same perk—stock options—that made Iacocca a rich man:

salary
commissions
bonus
stock-option plan

Salary. The first item to be negotiated is salary. Focus on it for two reasons: (1) because it usually constitutes the largest portion of the total compensation package, and (2) fringe benefits are usually tied to salary. Negotiate the maximum salary possible, one at least near the upper level of the grade classification or category your job is positioned at, so that any raise will push you into a new grade level and almost automatically guarantee you a promotion. When negotiating your compensation package for a new job, future raises are going to be calculated on the basis of your *entrance salary,* so it is doubly critical that you get the best deal possible at the outset!

Commissions. Sometimes, especially in a sales position, a commission may be paid in lieu of salary. Your strategy here is to negotiate the maximum percentage commission rate, for example, 10% of your sales. If you are less than confident of earning your target commissions, regardless of whether you consider the economy to be sluggish or the product as seasonal, you should negotiate a trade-off between the percentage commission rate (for example, reduce it from 10% to a 8%) and a guaranteed minimum salary payable as a monthly draw. Be very reluctant to put a cap on your earnings as part of any trade-off.

Bonus. Another cash item to be negotiated is bonuses. This benefit usually stems from your individual performance or the collective efforts of the firm or one of its divisions. Sometimes a cash bonus will even exceed salary. A friend of mine, Bill Mailer, earned such a bonus when he sold a nuclear-power generator to a large northeastern public utility. Nobody except Bill thought he could earn a cash bonus ($270,000) equal to nine times his salary of $30,000 until it came time to pay it to him. Use this skepticism to your advantage. If your employer doesn't think you can earn a bonus, ask, "What harm is there then in including it in my compensation package?" And if you do earn it, both you and the firm benefit.

Stock-option plan. You could do as Lee Iacocca did and negotiate stock options, trading off sweat equity for shares in the firm. Stock options are popular when you work for a firm in a survival or rapid-growth-oriented posture. You should negotiate stock options in addition to your salary (not the symbolic gesture of Iacocca), thus giving yourself the best of both worlds: a big salary and an opportunity to buy shares at a low price.

OTHER NEGOTIABLE ITEMS

Fringe benefits: The next items to negotiate are the fringe benefits. Before negotiating the particulars, however, you need to decide whether your goals are immediate or long-range. The impact on your finances will vary accordingly. If you want to maximize immediate rewards, negotiate things like medical and dental insurance, vacations, company payment of assorted expenses such as children's education costs, the portion of your home that is used for business purposes, or perhaps noninterest loans. Negotiate

109

long-range benefits like annuities, life insurance policies with cash values that accrue to you even after you leave the firm, retirement and savings plans, and stock options. Although the dollar value of both short-term and long-term perks may be the same in the year the perk is earned, a longer-term fringe benefit may prove considerably more valuable (and thus have a higher current value in your calculations) when you figure in the effects of annual compounding, inflation, and your future tax status.

Negotiate to control funds put aside for you as fringe benefits. Blind faith can be extremely costly. Suppose that the trustee of a profit-sharing plan decides to buy permanent life insurance (with a cash value) with the money in the fund. You may not need the life insurance in the first place. However, if you are, say, forty-one years and plan to retire at sixty-five, this decision made on your behalf, with your vested funds but without your say-so, is a monumental one. If the annual premium for a $152,000 policy is fixed at $2698, the cash value at retirement will be $40,000. If the trustee had instead decided to invest the funds in some conservative option, say a bank savings account that paid 5 percent, the amount of money in the account at retirement would be $120,000. Two key questions: Is the $80,000 differential in your plan too high a price to pay for the $152,000 in death protection? Couldn't the trustees do better by investing your money at more than 5%? The answer to both these questions is yes. This illustrates why you must negotiate as to how the funds put aside on your behalf are invested.

Don't worry about what everyone else is doing—do what is best for you. Consider the LTV bankruptcy, in which retirees lost some of their benefits. This alerted a friend of mine, Rose Flarrety, to inquire into her company's retirement policy. She discovered, after reading the appropriate documents and consulting an attorney, that the retirement benefits she had been promised and was counting on could in fact be modified by the company. The next day Rose was sitting in front of her company's personnel director, Ben Wilder, explaining her fears. "It'll never happen," he assured her. "We're in too good financial shape." Rose agreed that it was unlikely, then said, "These benefits are all I have coming. I can't afford to risk them. I want you to transfer my funds to the trust administrator on this letterhead." Understandably, Ben almost fell out of his chair. There was a provision in the company retirement plan that allowed the transfer of vested funds to another authorized trustee, but to his knowledge it had never been exercised. "Don't do it, Rose, it will set a precedent." "To hell with precedents, Ben," she replied, "it's my retirement I care about!"

Relocation: To further illustrate the range of benefits you can negotiate, consider the possibility that you are asked to relocate. Regardless of whether you are a new or current employee of a firm, you shouldn't forget to negotiate any possible benefits associated with this. Don't rely on the presumed goodwill of your employer to "make you whole," as they say; specify in your negotiations precisely what you expect. And get it in writing. Here is a list of benefits that could be negotiated by employees being relocated.

• Ask your firm to buy your home or condo from you. This immediately relieves you of the hassles involved in

111

the sale of your property. Many enlightened employers feel it is worth it to them to free their workers from extraneous worries so they can concentrate on their job. Many companies engage firms that specialize in purchasing homes from transferred employees. But a word of warning: these firms often lowball the price they'll pay for your home, so it could be to your advantage to search for another buyer. Usually these offers have a deadline by which the deal must be accepted or rejected; use the intervening time to try to find a buyer yourself.

• If your company won't buy your home, ask the firm to make the principal and interest payments for you until you're able to sell it.

• Ask your firm to lend you, at a rate lower than the prevailing market, the difference between the down payment for your new home and the net amount you receive from the sale of your old one.

• Ask your firm to lend you the difference between the interest and principal on the loan at your old location and your new one.

• If you are renting, ask your firm to pay the difference between your rent in your old location and your new one.

• If you are renting and plan to buy a home, ask the firm to pay the difference between your rent at the old location and the debt service on the new one.

• Make sure all your costs such as travel, hotels, food, and moving van expenses are paid. You also want your company to pay for hotel and food until you are settled in your new residence.

HOW TO DOUBLE YOUR TAKE-HOME PAY

You can double your take-home pay without an increase in salary by negotiating trade-offs and cash options such as bonuses and awards (special performance incentives) that are not part of a fixed salary. For instance, you could bargain for a special award of $1000 if you are able to sell a difficult customer. Or you could offer to reduce costs by negotiating to purchase a product at a lower price from a supplier when everyone else failed. Why not approach your boss and tell him or her that for $25,000 you will take on a special project and show how to streamline another department's materials-handling system, an area that is not within your career path and with which you won't get involved unless you receive special compensation. Don't be afraid to take on unusual tasks if you're sure you can cope with them. Don't be afraid to negotiate additional compensation in anticipation of your achieving them. The more skeptical your boss is of your chances of achieving the goal, the greater should be the incentive award you should negotiate.

You can also double your salary by negotiating with your employer and, indirectly, with the Internal Revenue Service! Here I must define your employer as a possible opponent because many companies are reluctant to change their computerized payroll-accounting systems to accommodate one person; it is easier to add a new employee to the system than to change one employee's records. Here, all you do is exercise your right (most people don't because, among other reasons, they don't want to call attention to themselves) *to take as many exemptions as you can justify,* thereby reducing your withholding taxes. File a new W-4 form and calculate the number of exemptions, at a ratio of one exemption of approximately $1000 of itemized deductions plus an exemption for each dependent. The purpose of doing this up front, before each year begins, is so that your withholding taxes will be based on the reduced anticipated taxable income and not on a higher amount before you changed your W-4. There is no sense letting an employer deduct extra withholding taxes and letting the funds stay on deposit with the IRS for at least a year when you could save, spend, or invest the money yourself. One caution: take care to pay at least 90% of the taxes you anticipate you owe the IRS by year end, otherwise you will have to pay a penalty.

NOTHING TO LOSE

There's a variation to the strategy of negotiating with your employer—what to do when you suspect that the performance-review interview is part of a plan to fire you! "Do not go willingly into the cold, dark night!" to paraphrase Dylan Thomas. Assuming you don't actually want to be sacked, you have one last chance to negotiate for your job. Sitting face-to-face with an interviewer who's about to fire you, perhaps ruining your career, you have a choice; either bow to his or her whims or hunker down and negotiate a better deal. Sure, it's a terrible situation—for both of you. Assuming he isn't a psychopathic sadist who enjoys such scenes, you have him in an emotionally exposed moment: he is probably looking for ways to persuade himself that you can be saved. Turn this chopping block into a starting block. Don't complain that you have been unfairly treated but rather that you have been underutilized, that you have not been in a position to demonstrate your true value to the company, that this situation is really a blessing in disguise since it will give you a chance to show your boss what you really can do! Negotiate with your boss on your indispensability, because you know you are indispensable. Get him or her to acknowledge that your qualifications far exceed the demands of your present job. Persuade him this is true; provide examples of how you have excelled, how you have served as a model and inspiration to your fellow workers, how you have always been loyal to his lead. Instead of firing you, he should be promoting you up the ladder!

If your reasoning is to no avail, don't agonize. Getting fired could be a blessing in disguise. I firmly believe it is better to be out of a situation—regardless of the temporary pain of departure—for which you are not suited, than to languish in obscurity, receiving token compensation increases and token promotions. Of course it hurts to be told that you are not wanted, that you have "failed." But look at the other side of the coin. Now you are free to pursue a career more suited to your talents. And you will be free to use your negotiation skills to make sure you're adequately compensated in that new career.

GET THE DEAL IN WRITING

Now I want to bring up a subject that isn't exactly pleasant but needs to be discussed. People lie. They will promise you the moon to have you come work for their company, agree to all your negotiating demands, and then—once you've moved your home and family halfway across the country and are ensconced in your new office—conveniently forget the terms of the arrangement.

A deal isn't always a deal, as Seth learned, much to his chagrin. After fourteen years working patiently with the same firm, he finally made it into the executive dining room when he was named regional sales supervisor. News traveled fast through his industry. A competitor decided to one-up Seth's company by hiring him away. After meeting with the vice president, soon to be his new superior, Seth decided to accept their offer of a senior managment position, big salary, bonuses, one month's paid vacation, and other perks. Two weeks later, when he showed up for work, Seth learned that the terms he had negotiated had only been "suggested" by his boss, not signed, sealed, and delivered. Top management had overruled Seth's deal and he had never been informed. The VP apologized profusely but claimed his hands were tied and that he only could offer a salary 30% lower than the previously agreed-on figure. Furious, Seth consulted an attorney who confirmed that there were only two ways to resolve the matter: sue the firm for violating an oral commitment or accept their new offer. Because of the bad faith shown by the new management, Seth decided he couldn't go to work for them. He successfully negotiated a settlement equal to the dollar value of one year's employment, something the company accepted only after being shown a draft copy of the proposed writ that would be served on its officers and directors.

Look at what happened to a fellow named Robert. He

left a very fine job with a top-ranking company to join an equally prestigious firm with the understanding that he would be groomed to become the chief operating officer of a major subsidiary. He was promised bonuses, stock incentives, and accelerated job advancement, none of which materialized as promises. He sued, and a federal jury awarded him $10.1 million in damages for breach of contract. The court ruled that the oral promises made to Bell constituted a binding contract. Robert committed a serious error in judgment, however, by trusting oral commitments without securing written guarantees—and it took him *five years* in the courts to rectify the wrong.

So be sure that the deal you negotiate with your new employer is put in writing!

A few years ago I gave a seminar for the National Association of Realtors in Chicago. A young student sat in the audience, listening intently and taking notes as I talked about various aspects of negotiation. Steve was a likable young college man and we struck up a correspondence. Putting into practice the principles I outlined, he succeeded in finding a job after graduation with a company in the metal industry. He finished school, took several months of deserved vacation, then showed up to claim the job he expected to be waiting. It wasn't. There had been an organizational shakeup, the person with whom he had been dealing was no longer there, and he had no written record of their negotiation and his job offer. In a mood of despair, Steve contacted me and we worked out a scenario. He put in a call to the president of the company—not at the office, where he kept getting brushed off by the secretary, but at the man's home. Steve explained his situation, stating diplomatically that he wanted the job he had been promised, or, if that wasn't possible, a better one. The president, impressed with Steve's initiative and preparation, agreed to see him. Steve got a better job than the one originally offered, and earned the respect of the president.

Steve was able to turn a defeat into a happy ending, but had he obtained a written record of the job offer and the terms, he would have avoided a lot of anxiety and lost time.

DISLOYALTY ... THE UNFORGIVABLE SIN

There is a fine line in negotiating with your present employer, and it involves loyalty. Under no circumstances do you want to be perceived as disloyal. Remember, if the negotiation is a success, you and your boss are going to be working together. So negotiate hard for your rights, but don't back your boss up against a wall and instill resentment in him or her—you might win the battle today but lose the war tomorrow.

A man I know employed a woman named Louise as a researcher to prepare presentations he made to clients. Louise felt she was underpaid and decided to do something about it. A week or so before a major report was due, she announced to my friend: "Give me a raise or I'm afraid I'm so overstressed I'll have to take a two-week sick leave." For my friend, it was like Russian roulette, except that all the chambers were loaded. He needed Louise to finish the work, and he cursed himself for leaving himself so vulnerable. What did he do? He didn't go whacko and he didn't fly into a rage at her. He swallowed his anger and went through the motions of negotiating with her, offering a smaller raise than she demanded but promising an extended vacation. He went overboard to pretend he was negotiating in good faith and bargaining hard with her. They came to an agreement. Louise finished the report— and I don't think it was more than fifteen minutes after it was in her boss's hand that he booted her out of his office for good. Don't try to be too clever for your own good.

THE WINNING GAME PLAN: A SUMMARY

Financial Situation: You want a better compensation package.

Your Goal: To maximize your salary and fringe benefits after taxes and inflation.

Your Strategy: Follow the same strategy when you're negotiating your annual review as you would if you were seeking a new job. Begin the interview by placing a current résumé—a marketing masterpiece—in front of the interviewer—even if you have been there for five or more years and the interviewer has your personnel file right in front of him or her. Direct the interviewer's attention to point after point on your résumé in order to get him to acknowledge your self-evaluation, thus inducing him to follow *your* agenda and not *his.* Demonstrate your indispensability to the firm. Suggest that you are eager to take on more responsibilities in order to further contribute to the growth of the company. Then introduce money into the conversation. This will tell you whether there is a basis for a deal and show him or her that you are a serious, self-confident person. The interviewer will probably want to avoid the subject until the end. The more reluctant he is to talk about money, the more you want to stay with it and force the issue. Now begin to sell hard, explaining why you and only you can best do this job and even more advanced jobs. Ask for more compensation than the company traditionally would offer. This convinces them to take you seriously by letting them know you take yourself seriously. Let them know that you earn what you get and that you deserve more.

Your options: Negotiate the first four items on this checklist in the order presented and the others according to your priorities:

Key Items

—Salary
—Commissions
—Bonus
—Stock-Option Plan

120

Other Negotiable Items

—Relocation
—Stock-purchase plan
—Profit-sharing plan
—Group term insurance
—Health insurance—basic
—Company car
—Parking privileges
—Legal advice
—Deferred compensation
—Group auto insurance
—Financial counseling
—Tax-preparation assistance
—Personal-liability insurance

—Vacation (with pay)
—Pension plan
—Deferred savings plan
—Medical reimbursment
—Health insurance—major
—Accident insurance
—Dental insurance
—Loans (low cost)
—Van pooling
—Adoption aid
—Personal education
—Recreation facilities
—Disability insurance

5

NEGOTIATING
A LEASE

IN TODAY'S WORLD of financial transactions, leasing plays an increasingly important role. Although the new tax laws will change matters somewhat (new depreciation tables and the loss of the investment tax credit), leasing will continue to figure prominently in many areas, including real estate, business equipment, and automobiles. Chances are that most of us will be a lessee (tenant), and perhaps also a lessor (landlord), periodically during our lives. Smart money understands the virtues of leasing, which was succinctly summarized by one multimillionaire who told me, "Buy assets that appreciate, lease assets that depreciate." Good advice! And, as with almost all financial transactions, you can make money if you negotiate the lease on your terms.

NEGOTIATE WITH THE RIGHT PEOPLE

Your time is valuable, so you want to be sure you're dealing with the right people: ones with the authority to make discretionary judgment calls, not ones whose instructions are to go by the book. The latter usually operate within pretty fixed limits. So, if you want to negotiate, avoid leasing agents who merely shuffle papers and carry messages to the owners, and deal with the owners of the asset or someone with the authority to make creative decisions.

Although our focus will be on leasing an office or apartment, the same principles will apply to cars, computers, or plots of ground, for identical issues are at stake: *the specific terms of the lease* and *ownership of the asset after the lease expires.* Each must be considered in terms of the marketplace.

MARKET CONDITIONS

How receptive a landlord is to negotiating the terms of a lease depends on whether you are in a lessor or lessee market. In a lessor market there is a perceived shortage of office or apartment space: "perceived" because that is exactly what it is. If you shop around, you will usually find just as good a place—possibly because the landlord hasn't done a good marketing job. In a lessor market there is also the perception that if you don't grab the place, someone is standing in line right behind you, ready to rent it, willing to sign the lease with his eyes closed. If that's really the case, so be it—but you should never be desperate enough to sign a lease before reading it and determining what concessions you can get, based on conversations with the landlord or with former occupants. If you are in a lessee market where you know there is surplus office or apartment

126

space because you can't help tripping over to-lease or for-rent signs, you will know that you can press for the most concessions.

YOUR GOAL

There is nothing arcane about negotiating a good lease for yourself. Like all financial transactions, it hinges on the cardinal principle of mutual self-interest. *Your primary goal is to rent the asset at the least cost to you and control its use while you are the tenant.* To do this, you have to persuade the lessor that it is in his or her best interest to do business with you—on your terms. You have to convince the land-lord that you are the ideal tenant for his asset—not only the best tenant but probably the only tenant willing to rent it. Make him think that it would be unwise not to lease to you, that whatever concessions he may have to make will be more than compensated for by your reliability and value as a tenant. Convince him that he'll never get a better deal than yours.

YOUR STRATEGY

I suspect you're thinking to yourself right now that this all sounds like a pipe dream. *How in the world,* you're wondering, *am I going to be able to be that persuasive?* Simple. You're going to let the landlord do all the work for you; you're going to let him or her tell you the basic terms, which you'll then "massage" to meet your goals. Just like a black-belt martial warrior turns the force and momentum of his opponent around to defeat him, so will you turn the thrust of the landlord around to your own advantage!

Here's how. You have found the property you want to lease. The first step is to gain control of the negotiating process. You do this by having the landlord draft a lease. In this way you will know instantly the terms he is looking for. You'll know how much he wants and how much he is willing to concede. He has revealed his hand.

Now it's your turn. Review the lease and also show it to an attorney, since the landlord's legal maven may have inserted some clauses you may not like. Amend the lease by inserting your revisions *in the margins*. Do not redraft and retype a whole new lease; you want to reassure the landlord that the changes are easily identifiable and you want to minimize the time that it will take him to approve the lease.

If you perceive that it is a lessor's market, your strategy is to convince the landlord that you are by far the best tenant for the asset—you make fewer complaints, do less damage, and so on. If the landlord still won't budge on the price, and you decide that you badly want to rent the apartment or office, then your tactic should be to ignore the asking rental figure, putting a discussion of rent aside for the moment, and begin to negotiate the other terms of the lease. (See "The Winning Game Plan" at the end of the chapter.) You could gain concessions that would reduce the cost of the lease, or gain other concessions that would convince the landlord that he would be better off if he lowered the rent. You may even want to put the "rush act" on him by convincing him that he should give you the deal you want—you are willing to sign the lease then and there; if he waits for another tenant, he might not get as good a deal.

If you are in a lessee market, bear down and negotiate the maximum number of concessions.

YOUR OPTIONS

Now you're ready to dig in and start negotiating, especially these three most vital aspects of a lease:

amount of rent
amount of space
duration of the lease

AMOUNT OF RENT

The amount of rent, the largest dollar component of a lease, is the most important item and should be negotiated first. If the rent is too high, stop negotiating for the time being. In order to negotiate the rent, you need to know how a landlord arrives at the rental figure he has quoted you. Generally that amount is calculated as follows:

cost of amenities
cost of completing work needed on the premises
operating costs
financing costs

target rate of return
what the rent market will bear

Once you know the lessor's cost figures, you can whittle down the rent to his lowest acceptable rate. Negotiate to reduce "What the rent market will bear" and "Target rate of return." You can approximate cost figures for amenities, preparing the premises for occupancy (painting, special lighting, moving walls, etc.), operating costs, and financing costs by asking commercial realtors or property management companies for comparable figures for other buildings. Tell them, if necessary, that you are considering purchasing a similar building. They will usually be glad to help you, since they are interested in additional management fees or sales commissions. You may even luck out and get a copy of a prospectus of the building you are considering, if the owners prepared one in order to sell it. Once you estimate these costs, you can calculate the difference between the total cost of operating the building and the asking rental rate—the landlord's profit figure. Your goal is to negotiate to reduce this figure; each dollar reduction is a dollar saving in rent to you.

The more you know about the landlord's situation, the greater the edge you'll have in the negotiations. If, for example, you are considering leasing a space in a brand-new building, and your lease will be the one that enables the building to reach a target level of occupancy, thus allowing the construction loan to be rolled over into a permanent loan at a much lower interest rate, use this leverage to negotiate even better terms. When the landlord zeroes in on this milestone, he is usually eager to get the deal signed—even at a lower rent. He may be willing to throw in more concessions than he might otherwise grant.

There are other rent items you should negotiate. If you're in a lessee's market, ask for free rent.

If you succeed in negotiating a number of months (even a year or more) of free rent, take it up front instead of tacking it on at the end of the lease. Otherwise it extends the duration of the lease, something you may not want. Some landlords prefer alternatives to free rent, fearful that after the free-rent period is up, a tenant will walk away. Instead, they offer to reduce the rent over the period of the lease, thus at least creating some cash flow. Negotiate to get the free rent up front, thus giving yourself the option to move if the building deteriorates or if the ownership changes.

Consider the possible trade-off of paying the total rent (or the rent each year) in advance in return for more rent-free months or a discount on the monthly rent.

You should not agree to pay for a possible escalation of real estate taxes, which, unless you specify otherwise in the lease, are ordinarily passed along by the landlord to the tenant.

AMOUNT OF SPACE

Negotiate to get the most square footage of usable space, eliminating common areas such as elevators, hallways, and lobbies or other areas that render you no service. Your strategy: Don't let this unusable space be figured into the square footage you lease. When the lessor says, "Then I'll have to increase the rental rate [for the usable space you rent]; someone has to pay for it," counter with, "Charge those costs to the other tenants who use them more, not me." It makes no sense to pay for facilities other tenants may use more than you will.

DURATION OF THE LEASE

Negotiate the shortest lease, with as many options to renew as possible. By so doing you can move whenever you want, while at the same time you reserve your right to remain for as long as you want. The challenge is to do this without any rent increases. A landlord will usually insist that "The shorter the lease, the higher the rent I have to charge you." Counter with, "Then you should lower the figure because I have no intention of moving for a long while." Don't agree to a higher figure.

OTHER POSSIBILITIES

After you have negotiated the three most important items in the lease—the rent, the amount of space, and the length of the lease—you must focus your attention on items such as:

cash
equity
security deposits
co-op or condo conversion

132

landlord default
reducing your landlord's options
special needs

Cash. In New York, Miami, and Chicago, lessors are offering a cash bonus to tenants if they sign more than a five-year lease. In Atlanta, a tenant in an apartment traded amenities such as membership in a country club, 25% of the finish-out allowance (for painting, wallpaper, etc.), and several parking spaces for $75,000 in up-front cash. Negotiate to get cash as part of your lease. I recently helped a client obtain $125,000, payable to him at the time of signing the lease. It was a simple matter of ascertaining the landlord's objectives, then putting together a proposal that satisfied them and served our own ends as well—in this case with an added $125,000 thrown in to sweeten the deal. Here's what happened. The landlord owned a large building with tenants such as a restaurant, a hair salon, and several retail shops. The leases were structured so that he received a proportion of their gross sales as part of the rent. So it was in his best interest to generate business. My client operated a small independent television station with a high-visibility format that invited people to watch and participate in the programming. The landlord realized that the stream of people moving in and out of the station would help generate sales in the neighboring establishments. It was worth a cash bonus to him to have the TV station situated in his building.

Equity. Increasingly, people are leasing with an eye to ownership. When transacting apartment or commercial real-estate leases, you should negotiate equity as part of the deal.

This option, however, is usually reserved for tenants who intend to lease a whole floor in an apartment or office building. Here are three ways to convince the landlord to seriously consider your request for an equity interest: (1) You are a key tenant—your presence will attract other tenants, (2) You are willing to trade off an equity interest in the building by paying the going or slightly higher market rental rate; in a sense, the difference between the lower rate you could negotiate and the market rate will be used to purchase equity in the building, (3) If the building is new, by renting space the landlord will be able to reduce his or her interest costs by converting from a higher-interest-cost construction loan to a permanent loan.

Patsy Hesplin is a fine example of how you can negotiate an equity interest. Her motto: "Just because everybody else does it one way doesn't mean I have to follow." "Patsy's way!" was the corporate leasing staff's toast in tribute to her, in celebration of the best branch-office real-estate-leasing deal in the history of her company. Patsy had always been skillful at getting good deals, obtaining maximum space for the least amount of rent. But this time she understood she had a very special opportunity. She was looking for space in a market that was in the midst of a commercial building boom, one that was overloaded with surplus capacity. She had an extremely valuable chip to play—her company wanted to relocate an expanding office and needed a lot of space. Because she was in a definite buyer's market, Patsy was able to negotiate a terrific deal. For about the same cost per square foot as she would ordinarily pay for rent, she was able to acquire an equity interest in the build-

134

ing. She discovered that the amount of space her firm wanted to rent would push the landlord over the minimum space quota at which point he could convert from a higher-interest-cost construction loan to a permanent loan, thus reducing his interest cost by $100,000. Her formula was elegant, simple, and irresistible in a market with excess office capacity: equity in proportion to the amount of office space her firm would occupy in the new building. She didn't disclose to the landlord that her target was equity equal to three years' savings in interest costs ($300,000) to the landlord. She found out this figure by requesting copies of the construction and permanent loan agreements, justifying her request, and, in the process, further confirming that she was about to sign a multiyear lease.

Security deposits. Don't pay a security deposit! Strike it from the lease. Stare the landlord down if he insists. Make clear to him that you have a longstanding history of paying your bills and that you are not the type who disappears in the dark of the night. You are just looking for aggravation when you pay a security desposit. This is particularly true with a residential lease. For starters, you have forked over a chunk of money that may earn you little or no interest. And you run the risk of not getting it back as promised.

How can you discourage a landlord from demanding a security deposit or not leasing to you? By making the landlord come to the conclusion that it's not worth his or her time to fuss about it. Do this by initially ignoring any mention of a security deposit. When the landlord presses you for it, ask for interest on it *equivalent to the return you get on your investments.* If this doesn't work, counter with,

"Okay, I'll provide a security deposit, but let's give it to an impartial third person to hold," for example a banker. "He'll decide if there are any damages to your property." Conclude by saying, "Why don't we go into the apartment [or office] and take some pictures so we'll know what constitutes 'damage' other than normal wear and tear." You can compare these pictures with ones taken at the end of the lease, so there will be no doubt if there is damage. And, by giving the money to a third party, you can insist that the funds be deposited in an interest-earning account. Another possibility is for the security deposit to be used as the last month's rent. Don't discard this argument even if the landlord points out that you could leave damages far in excess of a month's rent and he wouldn't be able to collect more dollars from you without taking legal action.

Look what happened in Los Angeles to Mookie Bahwana and you will see why I say, avoid security deposits if possible. He rented an apartment, not knowing he could have negotiated to forgo prepayment of a security deposit plus the last month's rent. At the end of his year's lease, as he prepared to leave, the leasing firm applied his full deposit to repair alleged damages and to clean the apartment carpets (which he had had professionally cleaned a few days earlier). Instead of the $2500 he expected to get back, he was stunned to see a check for $900. No amount of yelling could change the leasing agent's mind. Only after he made good his threat to organize a rent strike did the agent agree to refund in full his security deposits. But you don't want all these hassles.

Co-op or condo conversion. This is an aspect of leasing

that can lead to ownership. You don't want to find yourself in a situation where you as a tenant are suddenly confronted with the inconvenience and financial hardship of having to deal with your building going from tenant leasing to condo or co-op ownership. The traditional clause in the usual lease allows the tenant three months after notification of conversion to decide whether or not to purchase the property. This clause is to the landlord's advantage. You want something else! You want to have the opportunity to be able to buy your apartment, for example, in New York, at below market or "insiders" price. And if you decide not to buy, you want a clause that obliges the landlord to buy out the remainder of your lease in the event of conversion. Your leverage: the rent you (and other tenants) pay to a landlord constitutes the cash flow that enabled him to finance the purchase of the building. Or, if the building is owned outright, your rent is part of the income stream. Exploit it. Your buy-out figure should be at least equal to the value of the future rent you would have paid had you continued to lease the apartment (or office) through the duration of the lease, plus moving costs and money you invested in leasehold improvements.

Landlord default. You also want to be protected from a third party such as a bank or a new owner disturbing you in your apartment or office in the event that the current landlord defaults on his or her mortgage. I know of a case in which the tenants were given three months to vacate because the bank that repossessed the facility intended to use the space to house a computer center. How do you as a tenant prevent this from happening to you? By inserting

137

a clause into the lease that forces the bank or the new landlord to buy out the remainder of your lease at a figure at least equal to the value of the future rent you would pay through the duration of the lease. You negotiate this into a lease by convincing the landlord that it is a meaningless concession, costing him zero dollars. Play on his ego. Ask him, "Is there any chance of your defaulting on your loan?" Get him to tell you that such a possibility is so remote that there is little or no chance of it ever occurring, "No way, not even a slight chance." Now reply, "Then you wouldn't mind inserting that clause in the lease, now would you?"

Reducing your landlord's options. You should negotiate clauses that will hold the landlord hostage in his own building, so if he should decide to sell it, you won't reduce your freedom and flexibility. Negotiate provisions in the lease that provide fixed rent with no escalator clauses, or continual exclusives on available space, both of which make it more difficult to sell the property. You must avoid becoming a hostage. The same logic applies to the possibility of eviction. Why make it easy for a landlord? Make him go through the lengthy and complicated eviction process. Don't agree to insert into the lease a clause in which you the tenant in effect waive all rights to the assorted statutes that ordinarily apply in eviction proceedings. A sticky negotiation point, granted, but one that is in your vital interest.

Special needs. Negotiable options can also include special amenities such as data processing and telecommunication services of use to a business, or personal needs such as medical equipment if you are handicapped. There are always little details that can slip your mind—until it's too late! Larry Samuels rented office equipment and computers. Everything was fine until the hot weather began and Larry learned to his horror that the air conditioning in the building was turned off over the weekend and his computer system was getting screwed up by the intense heat. It was too late. He was trapped, and for the duration of the lease he was obligated to pay a special fee to his landlord to have his offices air conditioned seven days a week.

Negotiate the minor requirements of your business, such as garbage pickup, which usually isn't covered under the traditional terms of a lease. A friend of mine, Harvey Kerman, negotiated for over a year with the owner of a Mexican restaurant to persuade him to open another one in my friend's five-story building. He finally succeeded. It was a grand coup. All the terms were agreed to, the documents were ready to be signed. And then the potential tenant asked, in passing. "Where do you put out garbage in the morning?" It turned out to be right in front of the building, in keeping with city ordinances—but not in keeping with the best interests of this restaurateur, who could well imagine the charm of his restaurant spoiled by a line of garbage cans. The potential lessee had spotted a problem at the right moment—*before the lease was signed*—and turned it into a negotiating issue. My friend, eager to have this classy restaurant as a tenant but not wanting to invest his bucks to secure him or lose a year's effort, reluctantly agreed to construct a low-cost special loading dock off to one side of the building for garbage collection.

REALITY

Leasing gets you to the bottom line fast. Every month, when you write or receive your rent check, you'll be reminded how well (or badly) you negotiated. It's just like any other negotiating opportunity—it calls for *preparation, patience,* and *perseverance.* Stick to your game plan and to your guns the next time you sign a lease and you'll be well rewarded!

THE WINNING GAME PLAN: A SUMMARY

Financial Situation: You want to lease an apartment or office.

Your Goal: To rent the asset at the least cost to you and control its use while you are the tenant.

Your Strategy: Gain control of the negotiating process by having the landlord draft a lease that will spell out for you the terms he is looking for—how much he wants and how much he is willing to concede. Review the lease. Amend it by inserting your revisions in the margins— do not redraft and retype a whole new lease.

Your Options: Negotiate the first few items on this checklist in the order presented, and the other items according to our priorities:

Key Items
—Amount of rent
—Amount of space
—Duration of lease
—Cash
—Equity

—Security deposits
—Co-op or condo conversion
—Landlord default
—Reducing your landlord's options
—Special needs

Other Negotiable Items
—Cleanup: before moving in
—Deposit—first month
—Interest on deposits
—Utilities
—Repairs
—Leasehold improvements
—Date of occupancy

—Refunds
—Access—hours and exits
—Fixtures
—Arbitration
—Cleanup: after moving out
—Deposit—last month

—Parking for cars or other
vehicles

—Penalties: late payment

—Option to renew

—Painting

—Subleases

—Appliances

—Equipment allowed

—Recreational facilities

—Rent control

6

NEGOTIATING TO BUY OR SELL ANYTHING

WHENEVER YOU buy or sell something you are in a position to negotiate for financial success. When you walk through the front door of an automobile showroom or scan the real estate section of the paper or inquire about buying a business, the negotiating process has begun. That's the precise definition of a negotiation situation: when two parties come together out of mutual self-interest to consummate a transaction.

Regardless of the product or service you are buying (or selling), your goals, strategies, and options will be the same; only the number of dollars involved—a car, a house, and a business are usually at opposite ends of the price spectrum—are different.

Negotiating a big-ticket item has its own special flavor. While it's not different in principle or application from any other kind of negotiating, the moves can be more precise, the perception of "friends" and "enemies" a bit more blurred, and the risk of financial loss greater. Be on your guard, always keeping a close lookout for the unexpected curveball.

Never be reluctant to take a hard-line approach when you

are negotiating to buy a big-ticket item. Put the other side on record right from the start that you are tough and don't easily part with your money. Choosing among buying opportunities means setting priorities and weighing the relative costs and benefits of each purchase. That's all. No mystery. And yet you'll hear all sorts of mystifying gibberish and arcane incantations whenever a high-priced item is involved such as the new electronic injection system of a car, the home-security system, or the laser technology of a firm. There is no such thing as a hundred-and-ten-percent-safe decision when it comes to a big-ticket item, only more or less comfortable ones. *Your goal should be to negotiate maximum opportunity at minimum risk, specifically, get the most (car, house, business) for the least price.*

YOUR FIRST BIG PURCHASE: A CAR

When you shop for a car at a dealership, you have a great opportunity to bargain. Don't worry that the salesman is going to look at you as if you were crazy when you start to bargain, or tells you, "That's the price, take it or leave it." Amazing things can happen if you only dare ask. For example: "I'll take this car, but I want a stereo tape deck and two free rear speakers." Sure, often the salesman is going to refuse to budge, which is why if possible you should deal with the manager or shopowner; he or she will be more motivated and has the authority to make a deal.

The car salesman is no different from any other merchant peddling a product. Especially with a car dealership, the fundamental truth of negotiation is always brought home

146

to me: Never take the price for granted! Never assume there is no room for bargaining. All you have to do is develop a winning game plan. When negotiating to buy a car, your game plan must be fixed in your mind or written in nonerasable ink before you visit the dealership to avoid the temptation of paying anything to drive out with the fastest, shiniest buggy in the showroom.

THE BIG-TICKET ITEM: YOUR HOUSE

Buying and selling houses is a specialty. Nonetheless, the basic principles of negotiating apply here. And, if you are like most people, buying or selling a house will be one of your biggest financial transactions, so you will want to be right on your toes when you get involved with the housing market.

Emotionalism has ruined more house sales than any other factor. It seems that when a deal on a house is about to be closed, there are more things that can get in the way than there are leaves on a maple tree. To get the best price when selling a house or pay the lowest one when buying one, there is no substitute for a quick deal—one that is closed only a few days after the purchase contract has been signed by both parties. Contingencies such as waiting for a buyer to sell another house, or arranging financing, only seem to bring out the wail, "Do I *really* want to sell my home?" or "Will this guy find something better and change his mind?"

The housing market has changed, with corporate relocation services playing a bigger role. They agree to buy a transferred employee's house after, say, a ninety-day period, for an average price based on two or three appraisals if the employee doesn't sell it himself. This forces the employee to try to get more than the average appraisal before the ninety days expire. If you are a buyer and you learn that an employee has been given such a deadline, you have a unique opportunity to negotiate the purchase of the house at a price slightly higher than the average appraisal and with many other concessions thrown in, such as owner financing and appliances. Once the relocation service gets its hands on the house, it will build a profit margin into it, thus raising the price. The time to negotiate a deal is with the owner *before* the service gets involved.

THE BIGGEST PURCHASE OF ALL— A BUSINESS

The American Dream means the economic independence of being in business for yourself. Who hasn't wondered what it would be like to call no one boss or not to have to answer to anyone but himself or herself? Buying a business can be more than just a fantasy, however; lots of people do it! So can you. And it will be a lot easier to keep the firm growing if you know how to negotiate the deal properly.

It's not usually easy to get a deal structured your way. You must exert effort to protect your own interests. Whether you're involved with a limited partnership or a private company as the major investor, you have to recognize from the outset that your objectives are going to be different

148

from those of your partners. Some investors want immediate profits; some long-term growth; some easy liquidity. In the past, some have sought tax shelters. *But whatever your objective, negotiate to protect yourself.* Don't let what happened to Sue Jackson, a former business associate of mine, happen to you. Sue discovered that one day when she needed cash, she couldn't sell a block of her shares in a business—no way, no how! You see, she bought the business on terms, and until she paid off the balance she couldn't raise additional capital unless all the money went to pay off the debt.

A business is unlike other big-ticket items such as cars or houses since it enables you to generate cash up front— cash you can use immediately thereafter to purchase the business or reduce your investment in it.

To do this you have to know your options. Consider this scenario. You've finally come up with the idea that is going to make you millions! You can visualize the penthouse suite, the yacht, the cases of Château-Lafite Rothschild aging in your cellar. . . . There is only one thing standing in your way, one minor obstacle between your idea and the fortune it is certain to produce—and that is cash! You don't have the money to build an organization to implement the idea. What do you do?

You have options. You could sell your idea to another firm, say for cash plus royalties. You could try to raise capital through debt or equity in order to launch your company without having to surrender control. Or—now hold your breath for this one—*you could use your idea to acquire an existing firm.* Sound impossible? Perhaps—but not for those who know how to negotiate. Here's how.

Identify a company (it needn't be too large) that best meshes with your idea. The basic thrust of this company needs to be sufficiently consistent with your proposal so that you can justify its purchase. You negotiate a deal to acquire the company, subject to your obtaining the financing. Now you find a lender or a venture-capital firm and make your pitch. You can sell off 49% of the equity and retain control. You have far more cash than when you started out, and you have four things you didn't have before; the *cash flow* of the firm to be acquired, its *assets,* its *track record,* and *debt or equity capital.*

Now let's say you invested in a company and you want to get some cash out of it, thereby reducing the amount you invested but not giving up any voting rights. Unlike Sue Jackson, you can raise cash if you are imaginative in your thinking and negotiate to sell part of the *future-income stream* of an investment, at the same time earning in excess of a 40% return on your investment. Here's how. When you buy a share of stock or a bond, your earnings are the dividends of the stock and the interest on the bond, plus any future appreciation in the value of the investment. You can negotiate to sell a piece of that future-income stream and potential capital gain for cash. This is the way it works:

You own a share of XYZ Corporation, which you bought for $45; it pays an annual dividend of $5, which can be expected to remain constant over the next five years. It is reasonable to expect that by the end of year five the value of that share will be $100. So after five years the combined return to you for dividends and capital gains is $80 ($25 in dividends, $55 in capital gains). How much is a part of that $80 worth in the marketplace? It's negotiable. But let's say you sell 33% of the future-earnings stream for $25. Now you earn, in the first year, $3.35 in dividends, $25 by selling 33% of your interest, $28.35 in total, or a neat 63% yield on your original investment of $45. And you still control the investment and 67% of its earnings.

The selling of future-cash streams goes on all the time. It's something mutual funds often do when they sell a portion of the rights of many securities. And if the big boys can do it, so can you! All it takes is for you to rid yourself of the chains and shackles of conventional thinking, quit imagining the only thing you can do with a stock or bond is buy and sell.

There are ways to even get a 40% yearly return on an investment. Sounds crazy. But it's possible. One way to obtain this kind of megayield is by negotiating with your partners so that, for example, you receive the earnings of the firm and they get all the tax advantages. Or, in a different scenario, you participate in a leveraged buyout, negotiating to use the acquired firm's cash flow and assets as a basis for financing, thereby enabling you to obtain a sizable asset at zero cash investment.

This is the way big-league dealmakers operate. And so can you.

YOUR STRATEGY FOR BUYING PRACTICALLY ANYTHING

If you want to buy a car, a boat, a house, or even a business, the best strategy is to show distant interest, as though you were just browsing; marking time. In truth, however, you have done your homework—you know what you want and how much you want to pay for it. If, for example, you're looking to buy a car, first dangle yourself as "bait" until the seller makes a pass. Let the seller pick the moment when he thinks he's hooking you. Establish a dialogue. Then reach into your pocket or purse midway through the conversation to pull out a bundle of cash or a check which you have planted there specifically for this purpose. By so doing you are telling him, "I'm here to buy." Finally, guide the conversation around to the specifics of what you want. By now you are also communicating to the seller both the seriousness of your interest and the fact that you are probably the only person in the world interested in buying his product. The trick is to get the seller to think you are the only customer for this item. This is how you subtly seize control of the negotiation. Keep the conversation going until you get the price you want—then, and only then, negotiate credit, cash, delivery date, or other key matters.

An ex-classmate of mine, George Armins, is a world-class bargainer. He had acquired the art during twenty years of practice in the coffee markets of his native Brazil. When he came to the United States, he was amazed at the simplicity of the American marketplace, how few people understood how to bargain or even dared to try. George, however, has refined his technique and he is a black belt when it comes to getting the best goods for the least price. He has added new tactics to his repertoire.

This is how he goes about buying a car. When he visits a dealership, he plays the perfect innocent, walking around, looking at different models on the showroom floor, some-

times entering one, sometimes peering beneath the hood—
but never acknowledging the salesmen who approach him.
After a good while of this, he asks to see the sales manager
(whose name he has learned the previous day, telephoning
the dealership to find out). He visits with the sales manager,
bypassing the floor salesman (and thereby eliminating the
salesman's commission in the final determination of the
cost of the car). As he chats with the sales manager he
discusses transportation costs, preparation costs, options—
everything but price. By displaying such sophisticated fa-
miliarity with pricing gimmicks and techniques, George
creates the impression that he knows what he's talking
about (sometimes he does, sometimes he doesn't), slipping
into the conversation the fact that he knew about a dealership that tried to get the customer to pay for preparation
costs even though the manufacturer had already paid for
it. Or he'll question the validity of a supposed "manufacturer's invoice," suggesting that the dealer is paying considerably less. Finally, when he's ready to get around to
price, George plays every card available to him—his friends
will be coming to this dealership to buy, his firm is considering a big leasing deal—to sweeten the deal a bit more.
It always works like magic. George walked away with the
best price imaginable. And all because he has refined the
rules of the game to his advantage.

YOUR OPTIONS

Keep your eyes and ears open whenever you're in the marketplace. Opportunities abound, but you have to know how to negotiate these factors:

price
credit
cash
delivery date
initial commitment
title

Price. If you are a seller, set your minimum price. If you are a buyer, set the maximum price and don't vary from it. This is your "last-resort price," beyond which you should not deal; it is the last price you put on the table before you walk. Don't worry about the cost of "comparable" items, including houses or firms, or what your neighbor paid for his car. And don't say, "I can get a better deal down the street—can you meet it?" Why not? First, because an informed buyer or seller will *know* the price down the street. Secondly, because the price down the street may not be the best one you can get. Also, be careful when you use an intermediary when selling a house or a business. Don't let a broker establish the price for you. Often the agent will appraise the asset at a lower price than it's worth in order to make it sell faster—a plus for him or her but a minus for you. Remember this example. Say you lower the asking price on your house from $100,000 to $90,000 on the advice

154

of the agent, who is receiving a 7% commission. You lose $10,000; he loses only $700. Who has lost more?

If you are represented by a realtor or business broker, make sure that he or she informs you of every offer. It is your sole right to refuse it. Determine the minimum net proceeds (sale price minus commission) that you want from the sale of the house or firm, but don't tell the agent this figure. If you receive an offer that doesn't meet your minimum, and if the agent is eager for you to accept it, suggest that he take a lower commission.

If you are a buyer, always set a maximum price before you get caught up in the heat of the bargaining process. After you have spent long hours negotiating the deal, and mucho bucks if attorneys are involved, it is too easy to say, "Oh, a couple thousand (or million) more—it doesn't mean much over the long run." Your opponent knows this and will, if he's smart, try to use it against you, knowing full well that you don't want to leave the table empty-handed. But think about it—he doesn't want to leave that way either! That's why it's so important to first agree on the price. That way you don't invest a lot of time, effort, and dollars if there is no basis for a deal. Your strategy: *No matter how much expertise you have in an area, go back to the fundamentals when you review your goals.* Before you negotiate, ask, "How much will this item cost? How am I protected?" And, if applicable, "When will it be finished?"

Charles wishes he had put a cap, a maximum price, on the deal. The irony in his case was that he is a real estate lawyer who negotiates dozens of deals with builders for other clients every year. Here's the scenario. Charles finally got his palatial home built, but it had come in three years late and only after ongoing legal hassles costing two and a half times the projected price and 300% over his projected interest cost on the construction loan. What happened? He had forgotten to negotiate two essential items: a cap on the cost of the house (he let the builder construct the house on a cost-plus basis) and a completion date. The builder was in no rush. Sure, the price of materials was rising, but he was covered. Poor Charles, meanwhile, had left himself in a totally exposed situation. He suffered, I think, from more than a touch of arrogance—he figured that he was an expert in construction negotiation and didn't have to sweat the details. How wrong he was.

Credit. When you use credit to make a purchase, you have a different negotiating agenda than when you use cash. For starters, your first task is to hide from the buyer the fact that you intend to use credit. Make him think that you intend to pay cash, even when you don't.

Here's why. The "democratization" of credit, making it almost universally available, is one of the great discoveries of the 20th century. Credit allows the economy to sustain levels of consumption and production that otherwise would be impossible. It allows individuals to make purchases they otherwise couldn't. *It helps the seller make his sale.* But it also costs him in the process. Every dollar of financing that he has to offer is a dollar that he won't directly receive at closing. And the dollars he eventually receives are likely to be worth less to him, even with the additional interest attached, because of inflation and "opportunity cost" than if he received them at the moment of sale. These are the economic facts of credit; the seller understands them!

All this means that a shrewd seller, whether he is selling

a car, a house, or a business, will adjust his price upward to compensate for the use of credit. But of course he isn't going to tell you that.

Clearly, there are going to be occasions in which you'll want to resort to credit. That's why it was invented. When you do employ credit, though, negotiate your purchase in such a way that you are protecting your right to the profitable aspects of the asset you are acquiring. You don't want your credit obligations, your debt service, to become so burdensome that you risk losing the asset or diluting its value.

Cash. Cash talks. If you are prepared to make your transaction with cash instead of plastic, you have an open invitation to negotiation. Do you know that every time you use your credit card, the merchant has to fork over a percentage of that purchase price to the credit card company? Most credit card service charges range from 2% to 7%, so negotiate to reduce the purchase price accordingly. There is another negotiating point in your favor when you use cash, you have to tread lightly here. Some merchants want you to pay for your purchase in cash instead of by check or credit card so they don't have to declare the sale as income for tax purposes. It's illegal, but if they don't declare the income, that's their problem, not yours. How can you ever know if a merchant declares the income if you pay by check or credit card? You don't. So if someone offers you a lower price if you pay cash, be sure to get a receipt marked paid in cash as proof of your purchase.

Merchants also prefer cash because they can spend, save, or invest it faster. So negotiate the price of your car, home, or business in such a way that the seller assumes you intend to pay cash, and then—only after you have a signed purchase contract—do you discuss, if pertinent, credit terms.

Delivery date. Stipulate a fixed limit to the length of time you deem acceptable to complete the transaction. One reason is that some buyers like to drag things out as long as possible, keeping you on the hook with an "option to purchase," for which they probably paid nothing, while retaining their money in the bank, drawing interest. And there are people who will quietly sell off the assets of a company through the back door between the date you set up the deal and the date it is closed. Whether as a buyer or a seller, your goal is to *control the asset.* Three months is the optimum period to close a deal; don't agree to more than six.

Initial commitment. When selling any item always protect yourself from a buyer who tries to whittle down the price at closing. You don't want to be left holding the bag! Lock him into the deal.

Here are three ways to do this. First, get a nonrefundable deposit, big enough to discourage the buyer from walking away at the closing. Second, make sure that the time between the signing of the purchase contract and the actual closing is as short as possible. Third, continue to market the item—a house, for example—and get backup contracts. You should even add a contingency to the first contract stating that if you receive a better offer, the first buyer must close within a fixed number of days.

My friend Bill Savage almost got squeezed. His house was on the market for nine months and he had already made a commitment to a builder to begin work on a new house when he found his buyer. The deal was set. And then, at the actual closing, the buyer announced that after further consideration he wanted the price reduced by $25,000 or he wouldn't proceed. Bill didn't have many choices at that point, as he tried to swallow his rage. He could (1) accept the discounted price, (2) walk away from the table, or (3) try to negotiate another price that would reduce the shortfall. None of these was very attractive. Bill sought my help. I learned after making a few well-placed telephone calls that the buyer had been refused a $25,000 loan the day before the closing. We solved the immediate crisis by Bill's agreeing to finance the buyer's $25,000 shortfall for a six-month period. Bill made the best of a bad situation.

Title. Make sure that the seller *owns* what you're buying! Sounds elementary, right? It should be. But, like all things, there are folks who have had to learn the hard way. Your strategy: Invest the time and money necessary to conduct a title search. If you are buying a business, diligently verify that you are buying all the shares and assets of the firm.

I never knew Phil and Alice Prentice, but I read about them in the newspapers after Phil tried to shoot the man who sold them their home. (Lucky for both that Phil was a poor shot.) Ten years after their purchase, the Prentices discovered they didn't have a valid title to their house. Since they had paid for it with cash, the title search traditionally conducted by the lender hadn't been made. They had received a *deed* at the closing, but, as they were to learn when they tried to sell the house, a deed wasn't the same thing as a *clear title.* They had bought a house from someone who didn't have the right to sell it.

159

RONALD J. POSLUNS

KNOW THE BUYER OR SELLER

You can never know the buyer or seller well enough, even if you have lived with him or her for twenty years. Arnie Cheeters learned just how sharp you have to be, and how well you have to know your opponent, from a most unexpected source—his own father. Arnie had always figured that once you established an emotional bond in a business relationship, you could let your guard down. His father, an old hand in the business world, knew differently! And he taught the lesson to his son in a dramatic way.

Arnie's father had built up a nice little embroidery firm. The company had supported the family, Arnie, and his two sisters, and now it was time for the father to retire. Since Arnie had been working with his father for a dozen years or so, he figured the old man would pass the firm along to him. Imagine his shock the day his father walked into his, Arnie's, office, closed the door, and explained that he was about to sell the firm. Arnie was stunned and panicked. Before the deal could be finalized, he scurried about, raised some capital, and offered to beat the competition's price by 10%. His father agreed. They shook hands. And, while Arnie's anger continued to smolder, his cagey father scolded him for paying twice the price he should have. "You should have negotiated. You always need to negotiate. You shafted yourself. All you wanted to do was beat the other guy's price. How do you know there even *is* another guy?" Arnie was shocked. On one hand he was happy because the firm was his, on the other he felt like a fool. "I wanted to teach you one last lesson before I let you out on your own," his father explained. Arnie had fallen for the oldest trick in the book—*a phony bid from a phony competitor*. Who would have thought that a man's own father would play him for a fool? Who indeed. That was exactly what the old man wanted his son to understand. Never trust anybody! Every deal has to justify itself on its own merits, so don't count on special connections or intimate relationships.

NEGOTIATING THROUGH AN INTERMEDIARY

With certain deals it may be advantageous to act through an intermediary. Buying and selling real estate or a business may involve brokers, and even when you buy a car you usually deal with a salesman—an agent, of the dealership. In addition, if the transaction is big enough, it can be emotionally difficult. So you must be careful. Although the agent is theoretically in your employ, hired to act on your behalf, his or her interest and yours won't always coincide. *Be sure that your broker is on your side.* They aren't always. Remember, their interest is in making a sale, and if this means lowballing the purchase price in order to attract buyers, or getting you to pay a higher purchase price than necessary (often by suggesting there is another prospective buyer waiting in the wings ready to top your offer), they've been known to do it! Either way you lose. Make your presence felt in this relationship, the same as in any other situation that affects your finances. Do this by "negotiating with the negotiator," right at the outset, to make sure that while you may be a silent partner in the actual deal, you are controlling the process through your surrogate.

Here's how to control the sale of your house through an agent:

• Be sure that your agent thoroughly understands your needs and objectives. You don't want to be just another "bub" who can't get past the secretary. Make the effort to get to know your agent and to get him or her to know you.

• Establish clear-cut guidelines for the agent to follow. Agree on the minimum dollar figures acceptable to you (or the maximum price you're willing to pay if the agent is brokering a purchase).

• Make sure your agent follows the same steps you would in a negotiation: research and preparation, formulation of a game plan, and setting up the right tactics to stay on track.

• Keep in touch with your agent. Read documents. Ask questions. Don't worry about being a pest—that's how you get results.

When buying a big-ticket item, *be extremely cautious if you decide to let someone else negotiate the deal for you.* Sounds obvious, doesn't it? But the courts and the financial press are filled with tales of woe in which supposedly savvy people learned to their amazement that something they had paid a lot of money for wasn't quite what they thought it was. As long as you dominate the negotiation process, no one can make a deal in your name unless it's a deal you want. Once you become too busy, or too indifferent, to do this, watch out—you are leaving yourself wide open.

162

THE WINNING GAME PLAN: A SUMMARY

Financial Situation: Buying or Selling Anything

Your Goal: Maximum opportunity at minimum risk. Specifically, to get the most of the product or service at the lowest price.

Your Strategy: Show casual interest, although you're just marking time. You are simply dangling yourself as bait until the seller makes a pass. Let the seller pick the moment when he thinks he has got you. Establish a dialogue. Guide the conversation around to the specifics of what you want. Get the seller to think you are the only plausible buyer. Keep the conversation going until you get the price you want. Then and only then negotiate credit, cash, delivery date, or other key options.

Your Options: Negotiate the items on this checklist in this order.

—Price
—Credit
—Cash
—Delivery date
—Initial Commitment
—Title

7

STAYING
ON COURSE

IT ISN'T ENOUGH to have a good plan. You have to stay with it. You can have the greatest strategy in the world, and the shrewdest tactics, but if you let yourself get led astray as you negotiate, you are a sitting duck. Any deal can be sidetracked, put on hold, led down a blind alley—sometimes without your even knowing it's happening. There is a simple way to prevent this, however: *Stick to your game plan.* Patience and tolerance are the keys—don't let your opponent wear you down or make you mad.

It's up to you to keep the deal on track. Here's how:

• *Ignore the bluffs and threats of your opponent.* Financial negotiating is not like a football game, in which you have to be flexible and constantly adjust to your adversary's moves. On the contrary, you have your agenda and game plan. If your opponent huffs and puffs and threatens to blow the deal, stay cool. Your goal is to get the best deal, not to win the battle of macho egos. If you can't control yourself, better walk away, because you have only a slim chance of success.

• *Don't cave in to unacceptable terms, even if your opponent tells you it's his or her best offer.* In your game plan you decided on the things that were unacceptable to you. Now stick to your guns! If the deal fails to include your minimum demands, it isn't worthwhile to you.

• *Don't leave the negotiating table until you are certain that your opponent is prepared (a whisker short of putting his job on the line) to recommend ratification of the deal.* There will be occasions when you are negotiating with someone who in turn must get approval from someone else to consummate the deal. You want to get as close to the decision maker as possible, or at least to the person who will present the deal to the decision maker. You must be sure that this person is totally familiar with the details of the deal, comfortable with the terms, and committed to getting it accepted. You don't want either the specifics or the spirit of the deal to get lost "in translation." One way to make sure is to prepare an informal summary of the negotiated deal and have it signed by your opponent—this is an important first step in determining that the other party will hold up its end.

• *Make sure your opponent interprets each clause in the agreement the same way you do.* Walk him or her through the deal, point by point, item by item, making sure you both understand things the same way. Not everybody is a quick study! This will also save possible problems down the road.

• *Trust your instincts—unless they tell you to depart from your game plan.* Be aware of changes in mood or direction from your opponent. If you feel something is wrong and you can't quite put your finger on it, remain silent and see

168

where he leads the negotiation. If your instincts tell you something is rotten, walk away from the negotiations. *Better to have no deal than to have to live with a bad one.*

• *Don't sign an agreement in which there is a last-minute change of terms not previously agreed upon.* It is always possible, when the agreement is drafted by someone else, that you will find a surprise or two at the closing. If they aren't to your liking, walk away from the deal. Don't count on getting something changed afterward—by then there is no incentive for the other side to do so.

Any opponent worth his or her salt is going to try to divert you from your game plan. Don't take it personally. Expect it and be prepared, as I have. About seven years ago the operator of a scrapyard repeatedly told my client and me that he could go "down the street"and rent another yard even better suited to his purpose than ours. I secretly obtained an option on the other property. At the next negotiating session he made his unacceptable demands, which we of course rejected. He stormed out of the room, announcing that the deal was off and that he was going down the street. The next morning he reappeared, soulfully saying that he had changed his mind, and meekly agreed to our terms.

MONITORING THE NEGOTIATIONS

Did you know that you could go bankrupt even though you earned more money this year than ever before and your net worth is at a record level? That's why when

169

negotiating a deal you want to carefully consider the implications of anything affecting your *future financial well-being*. The deal you close today could make or break a totally unrelated one ten years from now.

There are four areas of concern:

after-tax income
net worth
financial flexibility
cash flow

SPECIAL NEGOTIATIONS

Certain negotiations require special game plans and tactics. Staying on track in these situations requires shrewd planning and quick reactions, for unexpected developments could ruin you overnight. In situations such as those discussed below, it is smart to negotiate, long in advance, agreements that are designed to go into effect as soon as a specified event occurs.

• *A marriage contract.* Sure, it strips away some of the romance but it's wise to negotiate who owns what and the financial obligations each party has to the other at the *beginning* of a marriage—to spare you the pain and added complications of having to do it on the other end should the marriage fail. A marriage contract is also a most effective and useful document if you ever go bankrupt, for an existent one takes precedence over assets that could otherwise be distributed in a bankruptcy settlement.

• *A living-together agreement.* Virtually the same as a marriage contract, it protects both parties from palimony suits should the relationship fail.

• *A divorce agreement.* Something of a new wave in the world of negotiating, this determines in advance how assets and property will be distributed in the wake of a divorce. It is a way both parties can protect themselves from much of the emotional pain of a divorce. A lady once asked me, "Why jinx the marriage beforehand?" My response: "You buy insurance and write a will, don't you?" Providing for a contingency doesn't mean it's going to occur.

• *An employment agreement.* This spells out your compensation package as an employee and your entitlements after you leave the organization. It covers such items as salary, bonuses, fringe benefits, grounds for dismissal, and your rights should you be dismissed or the company ownership changed.

• *A business buy-sell agreement.* This agreement details the terms by which partners in an enterprise can buy out each other's interest. At its simplest, it is like two children dividing a pie; since each is suspicious of the other's share, they agree that one will make the division and the other will choose which part he wants. A buy-sell can be set up so if Partner One makes a buyout offer, Partner Two automatically has the right to exercise the terms of that offer to buy out Partner One. This agreement ensures an automatic transaction process with a minimum of emotional and financial turmoil.

*   *   *

Negotiating contingency agreements in advance is extra work and expense, but it's more than worth it. You don't want to suddenly find yourself in an exposed position, especially if you're in the process of putting together other deals that could be compromised because of personal complications.

8

ENJOY
THE REWARDS

CONGRATULATIONS! You've done it. You've negotiated a terrific deal!

It wasn't easy. You had to prepare. Do your homework. Devise a strategy. Execute your tactics. Stay on track. But now it's done. Few victories are more satisfying than that of negotiating the best deal possible, shaking hands at the closing, and walking away from the table with a signed contract.

Yes, it's done—but it isn't over!

Even with an iron-clad, tightly written, legally airtight contract, you still have to make sure the agreement is worth the paper it's written on. Now you and your opponent have got to live with the terms of the deal, and that isn't always as easy as it can seem at the closing.

As long as you continue to owe someone money, or vice versa, the negotiations continue. True, they're of a different sort—now it's more a matter of maintaining a relationship rather than structuring one from scratch. *But it still requires attention and diligence.* Is your opponent going to live up to the terms of the deal? Even if you've built in performance guarantees and penalties, sometimes it's cheaper to walk away from a project than to abide by its obligations.

As the terms of the deal are met, each contracting party still has leverage to control events. For example, "The check is in the mail" is the classic delaying tactic for individuals. But there are even better ways to avoid repaying a debt— look at the "developing" nations if you want to see how it is possible to borrow billions of dollars without any serious intention of repaying them. Your opponent can quibble about definitions, arguing that his understanding of certain terms is different from yours. Anything that hasn't been explicitly specified is subject to tug and pull as both sides test each other.

A negotiated document is like a marriage—it is a living entity that has to survive both the good and the bad times without collapsing. So stay alert; don't get fat and lazy. The route from game plan to document is the road to financial success, but you haven't actually reached your destination until that last dollar is in your pocket. By then, if you've become a master player, you'll already be halfway toward your next deal, perhaps with the same opponent. Good luck!